Christmas 1985

from Britta & Björn

Cakes Cookies & Bread from Sweden

Görel Kristina Näslund

ICA bokförlag Västerås

Coverphotos
*Front: A festive Swedish coffee table may offer
mazarins, lingon cake (seen on the white cutt-
ing board), piped cookies, Grandma's jelly
cookies and oatmeal lace cookies. Usually there
is also a fancy party cake like this strawberry
cream cake.*

*Back: Christmas time in Sweden brings special
delicacies like saffron bread and gingersnaps
(in the basket) and sugary, thinwalled rosettes
or "struvor".*

© 1985 Görel Kristina Näslund och ICA-
förlaget AB Västerås
Cover: Ulf Lindahl
Drawings: Håkan Carheden
Photos: Hans B. Eriksson, Kent Jardhammar,
Olle Åkerström
Coverphotos: Olle Åkerström
Typesetting: Ljungbergs Sätteri, Köping
Printed in Sweden by Centraltryckeriet, Borås
1985
ISBN 91-534-0908-6

Contents

Foreword

The other day I went to my godchild's christening. Right after the traditional church ceremony, we all took part in another ceremony just as traditional: the Swedish coffee table. It was served at the farmhouse of the baby's grandparents. This being an old-fashioned country home, nothing was missing at the coffee table. It opened, as it should open, with sweet yeast bread and a couple of cakes. With our second cup of coffee we had a number of delicious butter cookies. The finale, enjoyed with a third cup of coffee and a glass of sherry, was the rich, fancy, cream-covered cake called *tårta*.

This kind of coffee table has for generations of Swedes been a popular form of entertaining. Every important occasion in life like birthdays, confirmations, engagements or jubilees has been celebrated with coffee and a smorgasbord of cakes and cookies. As soon as a friend knocked on your door, you made him or her coffee and brought out a large number of cakes and cookies.

The older generation still adheres to this custom, while younger people more seldom follow it. Coffee is still the favorite stimulant, of course, and the drink best suited for entertaining and for celebrating events big and small, but today it is usually served with just a cake or a few cookies, or perhaps a tårta, depending on the occasion.

This book presents a collection of favorite Swedish recipes covering popular kinds of bread, sponge-cakes, cookies, pastries and fancy cakes. You can use it to compose your own Swedish coffee table. At the end of the book you will find recipes for Swedish *limpa* and other tasty bread.

Maybe you have been served goodies during a stay in Sweden and will want to try your hand at baking these yourself at home. Or perhaps you are living in Sweden for a time and wish to bake something Swedish. I hope that these recipes will be of good use to you.

Görel Kristina

Things to Remember When Using the Recipes

All the Swedish recipes presented in this book have been carefully worked out and tested in the United States using American standard measures and ingredients. However, the recipes can just as well be used in any other country. Only remember to do exactly as the recipe tells you. It is especially important that the flour is measured carefully.

Flour used in the recipes is always white, all-purpose wheat flour except when otherwise indicated. The sugar used is always white castor sugar, except when otherwise stated.

When using this book, please note that:

- all measures are level
- flour is measured by sifting into the measure cup and leveling off
- eggs used should be graded "large"
- all baking is done in a preheated oven

Measures

In this book measures are given both in grams and ounces, deciliters and cups. Some of the measures are translated into round figures as it would be too inconvenient to have to deal with e.g. fractions of an ounce.

The measures used in Sweden are spice spoon, teaspoon, tablespoon, milliliter (ml), deciliter (dl), liter (l), gram (g), and kilogram (kg).

The following table is for those who wish to translate Swedish measurements into the nearest convenient American equivalent and vice versa.

1 spice spoon = 1 ml
1 teaspoon = 5 ml
1 tablespoon = 15 ml = 3 teaspoons = 15 fluid g = ½ fluid ounce (oz.)
1 dl = 100 ml = 6 ⅔ tablespoons = 100 fluid g = 3 ½ fluid oz.
1 liter = 10 dl = 1 fluid kg = 2.2 fluid pounds
1 kg = 1000 g = 2.2 pounds

1 oz. = 28.35 g
1 pound (1b) = 16 oz. = 454 g
1 U.S. cup = 16 fluid oz. = 454 fluid g = 2.27 dl

1 inch = 2.54 centimeters

The British fluid ounce is 1.04 times the American ounce.
To convert grams to ounces, multiply the grams by 0.035.

Oven temperatures

All temperatures are stated both in °Fahrenheit
and °Centigrade (Celsius).

To convert Centigrade into Fahrenheit, multiply by 9, divide by 5 and add 32.

To convert Fahrenheit into Centigrade, subtract 32, multiply by 5 and divide by 9.

Conversion Table (round figures)

°Fahrenheit	°Centigrade
212 to 300	100 to 150
350 to 425	175 to 225
475	250
525	275

Glossary

This glossary includes some Swedish groceries and other things. It also gives the Swedish translation of some words.

Things marked with * may in the United States be ordered from Maid of Scandinavia, 3245 Raleigh Avenue, Minneapolis, Minnesota 55416.

Almonds, *mandel.* Whole, slivered, sliced, chopped or ground almonds are frequently used for cakes, cookies and pastries in Sweden. Very often the almond flavor is enhanced by the addition of one or two grated bitter almonds, a nut not for sale in the U.S. because of its poisonous quality when taken in too large a quantity. Almond extract may be substituted for bitter almonds. Store almonds in tightly closed container in refrigerator.

To blanch almonds, drop them into a small saucepan with water. Bring to a boil and let cook for a minute. Drain and rinse with cold water. Squeeze each almond between your thumb and forefinger and the almond will slide out of its skin.

Spread the almonds on baking sheet and dry for a few minutes in a 175°C (350°F) oven.

To grind almonds, either use an almond grater obtainable in some specialty shops, or, which is quicker, use an electric blender: drop 1 dl (½ cup) almonds at a time into blender and whirl for about half a minute, or till pulverized.

To chop almonds, put them on chopping board. Use a French chef's knife and hold the tip of the knife to the board with one hand, move the handle up and down and from side to side until the almonds are the desired size.

Almond paste, *mandelmassa.* Made from 50 percent ground almonds and 50 percent sugar.

Ammonium carbonate, bakers' ammonia or salt of hartshorn★, *hjorthornssalt.* Formerly obtained from deer's antlers, this old rising agent is still popular in Sweden because it gives a special delicate texture to rolls and cookies. During baking it will emit a faint odor of ammonia, but this disappears and leaves no trace in the taste of the finished product. Buy powdered ammonium carbonate at the drugstore or delicatessen.

All-purpose flour, *vetemjöl.* Note that in this book flour is measured by sifting into the cup and leveling off. One dl flour, sifted into the measuring cup, weighs about 50 g. One cup of flour weighs 100 g.

One dl flour scooped up from the flour bag, as is mostly done in Sweden, weighs 60 g (1 cup weighs about 130 g).

Baking powder, *bakpulver*

Baking soda, *bikarbonat.* Used for ginger snaps.

Bread, *bröd*

Bread crumbs, *ströbröd.* In Sweden used to sprinkle cake pans.

Brown sugar, *farinsocker*

Bun, *bulle*

Butter, *smör.* To cream butter and sugar, leave the butter at room temperature for an hour to soften, then add sugar and beat with electric hand beater until soft and creamy.

Cardamom★, *kardemumma.* The dark brown seeds inside the three-walled white cardamom pod have a sweet aromatic flavor. The principal spice in sweet yeast bread, cardamom comes both whole and ground. For the nicest, freshest flavor, pound the seeds yourself with mortar and pestle. Twenty whole cardamom – pods removed and brown seeds crushed – equal 1 teaspoon ground cardamom.

Chocolate, *choklad.* To melt chocolate, put it in a small, thinwalled bowl. Place this in a saucepan with simmering water, remove from burner and set aside for a few minutes till melted.

Cinnamon, *kanel*

Coffee, *kaffe.* Swedish coffee is mostly brewed from finely ground beans. Instant coffee is not commonly used.

Cookie, *småkaka*

Cream, *grädde.* Light cream is called *kaffegrädde*; whipping cream is *vispgrädde.*

Egg, *ägg*

Flour, *mjöl.* The Swedish market offers a wide variety of flours and flour mixes. The flours used in this book are all-purpose flour, graham flour and rye flour.

Ginger, *ingefära*

Graham flour, *grahamsmjöl.* Wholemeal flour of wheat. Do not sift this flour into the measuring cup. Instead scoop it up from the flour bag. One dl graham flour weighs 60 g, (1 cup weighs about 130 g).

Krumkake iron★, *rånjärn.* Used for making traditional, cigarshaped pastries (pp. 53, 57).

Milk, *mjölk*

Pastry, *bakelse.* Similar to a small, individual fancy party cake.

Pearl sugar★, *pärlsocker.* This white, coarse, granular sugar is commonly used for decorating buns, cookies and pastries.

Platt pan★, *plättpanna.* Primarily a pancake pan, the *plättpanna*, a cast iron griddle with seven shallow depressions, is also used for cookies and pastries (pp. 42, 49).

Pomeransskal. Buy this, the dried peel of bitter oranges, at a Scandinavian delicatessen. Before using, cook in water till soft. Discard the white part and chop the yellow peel finely.

Rice paper, *oblatpapper.* (See wafer paper).

Saffron, *saffran.* A golden spice used at

Christmas time to flavor sweet yeast bread.

Sandbakelse tins★, *sandbakelseformar*. Small fluted tartlet tins used to make *sandbakelser*, almond-flavored tart shells.

Swedish punch, *punsch*. Well-assorted liquor stores in the United States carry this sweet liquor made with arrack.

Syrup, *sirap*. Swedish syrup is very thick and sweet. American dark corn syrup may be substituted but better still is the English Golden Syrup available at good supermarkets and delicatessen.

Rye flour, *rågmjöl*

Rosette iron★, *krustadjärn*. Used for making thin, crisp, sugared pastries (page 52).

Vanilla sugar★, *vaniljsocker*. Small cans of vanilla sugar may be obtained at a good delicatessen. Or make it yourself: split a vanilla bean and bury it in a jar with one cup powdered sugar. Seal and set aside for 2 to 3 weeks.

Wafer rack★, *bakelseställ*. A large aluminum half cylinder used in pastry baking.

Wafer paper★, *oblatpapper*. A thin, white, edible paper made of rice flour. Used for special kinds of almond pastries (page 50).

Yeast, *jäst*. Most Swedes use fresh yeast for their dough because it gives the best taste.

Sweet Yeast Bread

S weet yeast bread is usually served at the mid-morning and afternoon coffee break. Cardamom, cinnamon and saffron are the spices used for this kind of bread.

Saffron is an exclusive, very expensive spice that colors and flavors a soup or a rice dish in a most wonderful way. It is grown mainly by poor Spanish farmers who would never dream of putting saffron in bread, but this is just what Swedes do every December.

Sweet, golden saffron bread is a must every December 13, Lucia Day, when the morning brings a blonde girl dressed in white, with a crown of candles on her head. This girl, Lucia, represents an old tradition; she comes with light and hope in the dark, cold Swedish winter morning and she always serves hot coffee with special twisted buns, called *lussekatter* or Lucia Cats, and ginger snaps.

Saffron bread, shaped in different ways and often decorated with dark raisins, is also served at Christmas time.

Sweet yeast bread may be shaped in many different ways. The picture shows a plain plait (follow the recipe page 16 and leave out the filling) and a butter cake (page 17).

Cardamom Bread
Vetebröd

1 envelope active dry yeast
   or 50 g (2 oz.) fresh yeast
½ dl (¼ cup) warm water
100 g (4 oz.) butter
3 dl (1 ½ cups) milk
½ teaspoon salt
1 dl (½ cup) sugar
crushed seeds from 20 cardamom pods
about 1.2 liter (6 cups) sifted all-purpose
   flour (600 g)

Filling
100 g (4 oz.) butter
1 dl (½ cup) sugar
½ tablespoon cinnamon

beaten egg

In large mixing bowl, dissolve the yeast in the warm water. In small saucepan, melt the butter. Stir in the milk and pour the lukewarm mixture into the yeast. Stir in the salt, sugar and cardamom. Gradually add the flour and work the dough until smooth and well blended. Cover the bowl and let rise for 1 hour. Stir together the butter, sugar and cinnamon for the filling.

Turn the dough onto lightly floured surface and knead well till smooth and shiny. Divide into 3 portions. Roll out each portion into a rectangle, 23×30 cm (9 by 12 inches). Spread with filling and roll up like a jelly roll, beginning at the long side. Place the rolls seamside down on baking sheet; cover and leave to rise till double.

Brush with beaten egg and bake in preheated 200°C (400°F) oven for about 20 minutes. Let cool on wire rack lined with a cloth; cover the bread with another cloth. Makes 3 large loaves.

The dough may also be shaped as below (but always leave to rise till double and brush with beaten egg before baking).

Scissored Loaf
Klippt längd

Cut through roll with scissors at 1 cm (½-inch) intervals. Pull the sections alternately to the right and left.

Twisted Loaf
Vriden längd

Cut roll in half lengthwise and twist the halves together.

Butter Cake
Butterkaka

Cut roll in 2 ½ cm (1-inch) pieces and place cut side up in buttered 23 cm (9-inch) skillet.

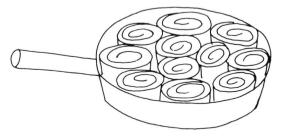

Cinnamon Rolls
Kanelbullar

Cut roll in 2 ½ cm (1-inch) pieces and place cut side up in paper-lined muffin tins. Bake at 200°C (400°F) for 10 to 12 minutes. Makes 3 dozen.

Saffron Bread
Saffransbröd

1 envelope active dry yeast
  or 50 g (2 oz.) fresh yeast
½ dl (¼ cup) warm water
100 g (4 oz.) butter
2 dl (1 cup) light cream
1 dl (½ cup) sugar
½ teaspoon salt
1 egg
½ g powdered saffron

about 8 dl (4 cups) sifted all-purpose
  flour (400 g)
beaten egg
raisins

In large mixing bowl, dissolve the yeast in the warm water. In small saucepan, melt the butter. Stir in the cream and pour the lukewarm mixture into the yeast. Beat in the sugar, salt, egg and saffron. Gradually stir in the flour and work the dough till smooth. Cover and let rise for 30 minutes.

Turn dough onto lightly floured surface and knead until smooth and shiny. Pinch off small pieces of dough; shape into 1 cm (½-inch) wide strips about 18 cm (7inches) long. Shape into any of the figures below. Place buns on baking sheet and cover with cloth. Let rise till double, about 1 hour. Garnish with a raisin in each curl and brush with beaten egg. Bake in preheated 200°C (400°F) oven for 10 to 12 minutes. Makes 20 saffron buns.

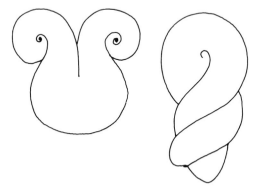

Instead of buns you may want to shape the saffron bread dough into any of the figures on page 18. Bake them at 200°C (400°F) for about 15 minutes.

Twelve Hole Kringla
Tolvhålskringla

Use half the saffron bread dough and divide into 2 portions. Shape each part into a finger-thick long rope. Braid the ropes so they form the figure to the right.

The Minister's Locks
Prästens hår

Use half the saffron bread dough. Divide into 8 portions and shape each portion into a 38 cm (15-inch) long rope. Curl the ends and place the ropes to form the figure to the right.

Christmas Cake
Julkaka

Use half the saffron bread dough. Divide into 7 portions and shape them all into long ropes. Roll them up; place one in center and the others around with the curls all in the same direction.

Large Lucia Cat
Stor lussekatt

Divide the saffron bread dough in 2 portions and shape into 45 cm (18-inch) strips. Place the two strips side by side on baking sheet and curl the ends in opposite directions.

The sweet golden bread of Christmas is flavored with saffron and given traditional shapes.

Danish Pastry
Wienerbröd

In Denmark and Sweden Danish pastry is called *wienerbröd*, or Vienna Bread, because Austrian bakers taught the Danes the Viennese technique of folding butter into a yeast dough to make a light flaky pastry with numerous tissue-thin layers.

1 envelope active dry yeast
or 50 g (2 oz.) fresh yeast
2 dl (1 cup) cold water
½ teaspoon salt
3 tablespoons sugar
1 egg
about 8 dl (4 cups) sifted all-purpose
flour (400 g)
350 g (12 oz.) margarine

In large mixing bowl, dissolve the yeast in the water. Beat in the salt, sugar and egg. Add the flour and work the dough till smooth. Roll it out on lightly floured surface into a rectangle of little more than ½ cm (¼ inch) thickness. Slice the margarine and cover ⅔ of the dough. Fold the dough in three starting with the plain part. Roll out the dough and fold again; repeat this three times. Put the dough in plastic bag and refrigerate for ½ hour.

Roll out the dough to a 50 cm (20-inch) square. Shape into combs, crescents or envelopes. Place on baking sheet, cover and allow to rise at room temperature for about 1 hour.

Brush with lightly beaten egg white mixed with two drops of water. Bake in preheated 225°C (425°F) oven for 10 to 12 minutes. Let cool uncovered on wire rack. Makes 25 pastries.

Combs
Kammar

Cut the rolled-out dough into 10 cm (4-inch) strips. Spread almond filling along center of strip. Fold each strip over lengthwise and press the edges firmly together. Cut in 10 cm (4-inch) pieces and make 4 deep slashes on one side. Bend the pastries slightly and place on baking sheet. Before baking sprinkle with chopped unblanched almonds and sugar mixed together.

Almond Filling: Stir together 100 g (4 oz.) almond paste, 1 dl (½ cup) sugar and 1 lightly beaten egg white. Beat until smooth.

Crescents
Gifflar

Cut the rolled-out dough into 12 cm (5-inch) strips. Cut each strip into triangles with 12 cm (5-inch) base. Place a dab of nut filling at the base and roll up toward the point. Bend the pastries slightly and place point down on baking sheet. Before baking sprinkle with broken flaked almonds.

Nut Filling: Stir together 100 g (4 oz.) butter, 1 dl (½ cup) sugar and 2 dl (1 cup) finely chopped hazelnuts.

Quick Danish Pastry
Enkla wienerbröd

225 g (8 oz.) butter or margarine
1 envelope active dry yeast
   or 50 g (2 oz.) fresh yeast
2 dl (1 cup) cold water
3 tablespoons sugar
¼ teaspoon salt
9 dl (4 cups) sifted all-purpose
   flour (400 g)

Filling
2 tablespoons butter
2 tablespoons sugar
1 teaspoon vanilla sugar or extract

Garnish
1 beaten egg
2 tablespoons finely chopped
   unblanched almonds

Soften the butter in room temperature. In
a large mixing bowl, dissolve the yeast in
the water. Add the butter, sugar, salt and
flour. Work the dough with your hands
until well blended. Cover the bowl and
leave to rise for 2 hours in refrigerator.
Stir together the butter, sugar and vanilla
for the filling.

   Turn the dough onto floured pastry
board and roll at once into a rectangle 30
by 40 cm (12 by 16 inches). Cut in 10 cm
(4-inch) squares, then cut each square
across into triangles. Spread each triangle
with the filling, fold the edges toward
center. Place in greased or paper-lined
muffin tins. Cover with a cloth and leave
to rise in room temperature for 1 ½ to 2
hours or till double in size. Brush with
beaten egg and sprinkle with chopped
almonds. Bake for 10 to 12 minutes in a
preheated oven 200°C (400°F). Makes
2 dozen. If desired, frost the pastries with
powdered sugar stirred with rum or water
to a thin glaze.

Almond Rolls
Mandelkubb

100 g (4 oz.) butter
1 dl (½ cup) sugar
1 egg
1 dl (½ cup) sour cream
½ tablespoon almond extract
   or 4 grated bitter almonds
½ teaspoon salt
5 dl (2 ½ cups) sifted all-purpose flour
   (250 g)
2 teaspoons ammonium carbonate

Garnish
beaten egg
2 tablespoons pearl sugar
2 tablespoons chopped unblanched
   almonds

Preheat oven to 200°C (400°F). In large
mixing bowl, cream together the butter
and sugar. Beat in the egg, sour cream,
almond extract and salt. Add the flour
mixed with ammonium carbonate and stir
just till mixed.

   Drop by large tablespoonfuls on baking
sheet. Brush with beaten egg and sprinkle
with pearl sugar mixed with chopped
almonds. Bake for 12 to 15 minutes.
Makes 14 rolls.

Nut Crescents
Nötgifflar

**1 envelope active dry yeast
    or 50 g (2 oz.) fresh yeast
2 dl (1 cup) warm milk
200 g (7 oz.) butter, softened
½ dl (¼ cup) sugar
½ teaspoon salt
about 8 dl (4 cups) sifted all-purpose
    flour (400 g)**

Filling
**2 tablespoons butter
½ dl (¼ cup) sugar
1 ½ dl (⅔ cup) finely chopped or ground
    hazelnuts
beaten egg**

In large mixing bowl, dissolve the yeast in
the warm milk. Add the butter, sugar, salt
and flour; work the dough with wooden
fork or your hands till smooth. Cover and
refrigerate for 2 hours. Stir together the
butter, sugar and nuts for the filling.

Turn the dough onto lightly floured
surface and knead briefly. Divide into 3
portions. Roll each portion into a 30 cm
(11-inch) circle; cut each circle into 8
wedges. Put a teaspoonful of filling at the
base of each wedge and roll toward point.
Bend the roll and place point down on
baking sheet.

Cover and let rise till double. Brush
with beaten egg and bake in preheated
200°C (400°F) oven about 12 minutes.
Makes 2 dozen.

Quick Apple Buns
Äppelbullar

These buns are good to eat, pretty to look
at and what's more, they are made in prac-
tically no time at all.

**5 dl (2 ½ cups) sifted all-purpose flour
    (250 g)
1 tablespoon baking powder
¼ teaspoon salt
1 dl (½ cup) sugar
1 egg
1 dl (½ cup) milk
100 g (4 oz.) butter**

**2 apples
1 tablespoon sugar
¼ teaspoon cinnamon**

Preheat oven to 200°C (400°F). In a large
bowl, mix the flour, baking powder, salt
and sugar. In a small bowl, beat together
the egg and milk. Rub the butter into the
dry ingredients; when crumbly, stir in the
milk mixture and mix quickly into a
dough. Flour your hands and shape into
12 balls, place on baking sheet. Peel and
cut the apples in wedges; press 3 wedges
into each bun. Sprinkle with sugar mixed
with cinnamon on top. Bake for about 12
minutes or till golden brown. Like all
quick bread, these buns are best when
newly baked. Makes 12 buns.

Streusel Cake
Strösselkaka

1 egg
2 dl (1 cup) milk
½ tablespoon almond extract
   or 4 grated bitter almonds
6 ½ dl (3 cups) sifted all-purpose flour
   (300 g)
1 tablespoon baking powder
½ teaspoon salt
1 dl (½ cup) sugar
100 g (4 oz.) butter

Topping
1 dl (½ cup) chopped hazelnuts
½ dl (¼ cup) sugar
3 tablespoons flour
3 tablespoons melted butter

Preheat oven to 200°C (400°F). Butter a
25 cm (10-inch) cast iron skillet or cake
pan. In small bowl, beat together the egg,
milk and almond extract. In large mixing
bowl, combine the flour, baking powder,
salt and sugar. Rub the butter into the dry
ingredients. When crumbly, add the milk
mixture and stir quickly just till dry ingredients are moistened. Turn into skillet.

   Stir together the ingredients for the topping and spread on top. Bake for about
20 minutes.

Cookies

S wedish butter cookies are almost as famous as
the Swedish *smörgåsbord*. To round off a lunch
or supper, there is nothing better than a fine butter cookie and a cup of well-made coffee . . .

Never hesitate to work a cookie dough with
your hands; it is the quickest way to a smooth,
well blended dough. In the basic butter cookie
dough recipe, the warmth of your hands is necessary to turn the mixture into a smooth dough.

If the dough is too soft to handle, chill it for half
an hour or longer before shaping. If the dough
crumbles, you have probably added too much
flour; add a few tablespoons butter and knead
well, then bake a test cookie. Always remember to
follow the recipe to the letter and you will have no
problems. Always bake cookies in the middle
third of the oven.

If you want to be sure, always make a test
cookie. Shape one cookie and bake it. If it does

not keep its shape, add more flour to the dough.

The recipes have all been tested and baked on baking sheet with nonstick finish; if you are using baking sheet without this special finish, remember to grease it. Do not put cookies too close to each other on the baking sheet as they always spread somewhat in the oven. After baking, let cool for a minute on the baking sheet, then transfer the cookies to wire rack to finish cooling.

Store cookies in clean, dry container with a tight lid. Butter cookies may be stored for a couple of weeks at room temperature, for 2 to 3 months in freezer.

Basic Butter Cookie Dough
Grundrecept för mördegskakor

The most common kind of Swedish cookies are called *mördegskakor* or "tender-dough-cookies". These short, tender cookies always contain flour, sugar and butter; by adding various flavorings and by shaping the dough in different ways, a variety of cookies can be made from the same basic recipe.

225 g (8 oz.) butter
1 dl (½ cup) sugar
5 ½ dl (2 ½ cups) sifted all-purpose flour (250 g)

In large mixing bowl, combine the ingredients. Use your hands and rub the butter into the flour and sugar. Work the crumbs between your hands; after a couple of minutes you will have a soft, well blended dough.

Fork Cookies
Gaffelkakor

1 quantity basic butter cookie dough
1 tablespoon vanilla sugar

Preheat oven to 175°C (350°F). Prepare the cookie dough adding vanilla sugar to the ingredients. Shape the dough into small balls and place on baking sheet. Press once or twice with a fork. Bake for 12 to 15 minutes. Makes 4 dozen.

The drawing shows the easiest and quickest way to make uniform size cookie balls: divide the dough into 4 portions, then shape each portion into a long log and cut in 12. Roll each piece between your palms into a ball and place on baking sheet.

The Strasbourg cookie dough may be pressed into small flat roses or sticks (page 43). The cookies can be decorated with jelly or dipped into melted chocolate.

26

Currant Cookies
Korintkakor

1 quantity basic butter cookie dough, page 26
1 dl (½ cup) currants

Preheat oven to 175°C (350°F). Prepare the cookie dough adding currants to the ingredients. Shape into small balls, flatten them slightly and place on baking sheet. Bake for 12 to 15 minutes. Makes 4 dozen.

Lemon Rings
Citronringar

1 quantity basic butter cookie dough, page 26
grated rind of 2 lemons

Garnish
pearl sugar

Preheat oven 175°C (350°F). Prepare the cookie dough adding grated lemon rind to the ingredients. Chill the dough if too soft to handle. Shape into long ½ cm (¼-inch) thick strands, place them parallel with each other. Cut in 10 cm (4-inch) pieces. Shape each piece into a ring, dip in pearl sugar and place on baking sheet. Bake for 8 to 10 minutes. Makes 4 dozen.

Chocolate Balls
Chokladbollar

1 quantity basic butter cookie dough, page 26
1 egg yolk
3 tablespoons cocoa
1 tablespoon vanilla sugar
1 dl (½ cup) chopped semi-sweet chocolate morsels

Garnish
slivered almonds

Preheat oven to 175°C (350°F). Prepare the cookie dough adding the egg yolk, cocoa, vanilla sugar and chopped chocolate. Mix well. Shape the dough into small balls and place on baking sheet. Garnish each cookie with an almond sliver. Bake for 12 to 15 minutes. Makes 4 dozen.

Brussels Cookies
Brysselkex

1 quantity basic butter cookie dough, page 26
1 tablespoon vanilla sugar

Garnish
pearl sugar

Prepare the cookie dough adding vanilla sugar to the ingredients. Shape the dough into two long logs the size of 3 ½ cm (1 ½ inch) across. Roll in pearl sugar and chill.

Preheat oven to 175°C (350°F). Cut the logs in ½ cm (¼-inch) thick slices and place on baking sheet. Bake for 10 minutes, or until golden. Makes 5 dozen.

Praline Cookies
Nougatkakor

1 quantity basic butter cookie dough, page 26

Praline
1 dl (½ cup) sugar
½ dl (¼ cup) chopped blanched almonds

Prepare the cookie dough. To make the praline, melt the sugar in skillet over low heat constantly stirring. When light brown and syrupy, stir in the almonds. Pour the mixture onto buttered baking sheet and leave to cool and harden. Break into pieces and crush them with mortar and pestle, or place them in plastic bag and roll with a rolling pin. Work the crumbs into the cookie dough. Shape into two logs 3 ½ cm (1 ½-inch) across. Chill for 2 hours.

Preheat oven to 175°C (350°F). Cut the logs in ½ cm (¼-inch) thick slices and place on baking sheet. Bake for about 10 minutes. Makes 5 dozen.

Checkerboard Cookies
Schackrutor

1 quantity basic butter cookie dough, page 26
1 tablespoon vanilla sugar
2 tablespoons cocoa

Prepare the cookie dough. Cut in half; mix one part with the vanilla sugar and the other part with the cocoa. Knead until well blended. Cut both the light and the dark dough in half and shape into 38 cm (15-inch) long logs. Place a dark and a light log side by side, then put a dark log on top of the light one and vice versa. Chill for 2 hours.

Preheat oven to 175°C (350°F). Cut the log in ½ cm (¼-inch) thick slices and place on baking sheets. Bake for 10 to 12 minutes. Makes 5 dozen.

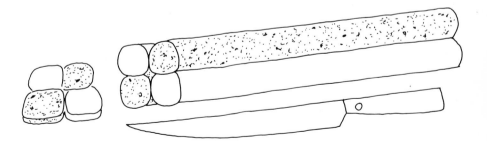

Jam Cookies
Syltkakor

**1 quantity basic butter cookie dough,
page 26**
¾ dl (⅓ cup) firm raspberry jam

Frosting
1 dl (½ cup) powdered sugar
about 1 tablespoon water

Preheat oven to 175°C (350°F). Prepare
the cookie dough. Shape into three 40 cm
(16-inch) logs and place on baking sheet.
Flatten them slightly and make a depression down the length of each log. Fill with
jam. Bake for 15 to 18 minutes or till the
edges are light golden.

Stir the powdered sugar with water to a
thin glaze and spread over the jam. Let
cool for 15 minutes, then cut the strips in
1-inch diagonal pieces. Makes 4 dozen.

Parisian Cookies
Pariserbröd

**1 quantity basic butter cookie dough,
page 26**
1 dl (½ cup) red currant jelly

Preheat oven to 175°C (350°F). Prepare
the cookie dough. If too soft to handle,
chill for half an hour.

Divide the dough into 9 portions and
shape into 40 cm (16-inch) long strands.
Place the strands three and three together
on baking sheet. Pipe the jelly in two lines
between the strands. Bake for 15 to 18

minutes, or until the edges are light golden. Let cool for 15 minutes, then cut the
strips in 2 ½ cm (1-inch) diagonal pieces.
Makes 4 dozen.

Vanilla Crescents
Vaniljhorn

225 g (8 oz.) butter
**5 ½ dl (2 ½ cups) sifted all-purpose flour
(250 g)**
3 tablespoons vanilla sugar

Garnish
sugar

Preheat oven to 175°C (350°F). Rub the
butter into the flour mixed with vanilla
sugar. Knead until smooth and well
blended. Chill the dough if too soft to
handle.

Shape the dough into small balls and
roll between your palms into crescents.
Place on baking sheet, bend the ends a
little. Bake for 15 to 18 minutes, or until
barely golden. Let cool for 5 minutes,
then roll the cookies in sugar. Makes 4
dozen.

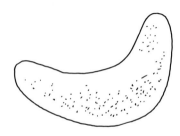

Nut Cookies
Nötkrokar

100 g (4 oz.) butter
¾ dl (⅓ cup) sugar
1 egg yolk
1 dl (½ cup) hazelnuts
2 ½ dl (1 ¼ cups) sifted all-purpose flour
  (125 g)

Garnish
1 dl (½ cup) semi-sweet chocolate
  morsels, melted

Preheat oven to 175°C (350°F). Cream the butter and sugar, beat in the egg yolk. Grind the nuts and add together with the flour, blend well. Divide the dough into 3 portions, shape each into a long log and cut in 10. Roll each piece between your palms into a crescent, place on baking sheet and bend the ends a little. Bake for about 12 minutes. Let cool. Dip both ends of each cookie into melted chocolate and leave to harden on waxed paper. Makes 30 cookies.

Berlin Rings
Berlinerkransar

2 hard-boiled egg yolks
2 raw egg yolks
1 dl (½ cup) sugar
225 g (8 oz.) butter
6 ½ dl (3 cups) sifted all-purpose flour
  (300 g)

Garnish
1 egg white, lightly beaten
pearl sugar

Preheat oven to 175°C (350°F). Pass the cooked egg yolks through a sieve. Mix with raw egg yolks, sugar and butter; stir till creamy. Add the flour and blend well. Chill the dough if too soft to handle.

Shape the dough into long ½ cm (¼-inch) thick strands, place the strands parallel with each other. Cut them, all at once, in 10 cm (4-inch) pieces. Shape each piece into a ring, brush with egg white and dip in pearl sugar. Place on baking sheet. Bake for 10 minutes, or until golden. Makes 5 dozen.

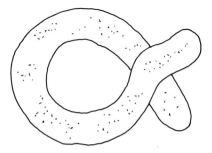

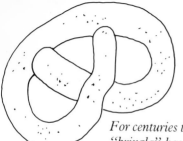

For centuries the golden "kringla" has been the symbol of the Swedish baker.

Karl XV's Kringlor

175 g (6 oz.) butter
½ dl (¼ cup) whipping cream
1 ½ dl (2 cups) sifted all-purpose flour (200 g)

Garnish
pearl sugar

Stir the butter till creamy. Add the cream and flour; stir quickly into a smooth dough. Chill for 1 hour.

Preheat oven to 175°C (350°F). Shape the dough into long, very thin strands and put them parallel with each other. Cut in 20 cm (8-inch) pieces. Shape each piece into a *kringla*, brush with water and dip in pearl sugar. Place on baking sheet. Bake for about 10 minutes. Makes 4 dozen.

Cinnamon Logs
Kanelkubbar

225 g (8 oz.) butter
¾ dl (⅓ cup) sugar
5 ½ dl (2 ½ cups) sifted all-purpose flour (250 g)

Garnish
1 beaten egg
½ dl (¼ cup) sugar
1 teaspoon cinnamon

In large mixing bowl, combine the flour, butter and sugar. Work the dough with your hands until smooth and well blended. Chill for half an hour.

Preheat oven to 175°C (350°F). Divide the dough into 6 portions and shape into 40 cm (16-inch) logs. Place the logs parallel with each other and cut into 5 cm (2-inch) pieces. Brush, all at once, with beaten egg and sprinkle with sugar mixed with cinnamon. Place the cookies on baking sheet. Bake for 12 to 15 minutes. Makes 4 dozen.

Finnish Sticks
Finska pinnar

Follow the recipe for Cinnamon Logs adding 1 teaspoon almond extract or 3 grated bitter almonds to the dough. Omit the cinnamon and sprinkle the cookies with pearl sugar mixed with chopped unblanched almonds.

Chocolate Sticks
Chokladpinnar

225 g (8 oz.) butter
1 dl (½ cup) sugar
½ tablespoon vanilla sugar
1 dl (½ cup) cocoa
2 egg yolks
4 ½ dl (2 cups) sifted all-purpose flour
 (200 g)

Garnish
175 g (1 cup) semi-sweet chocolate
 morsels, melted

In large mixing bowl, combine the butter, sugar, vanilla sugar, cocoa and egg yolks. Stir until creamy. Add the flour and work the dough until well blended. Chill for 1 hour.

Shape the dough into a bar, 2 by 5 by 35 cm (¾ by 2 by 15 inches). Chill for 2 hours.

Preheat oven to 175°C (350°F). Cut the bar in ½ cm (¼-inch) thick slices and place on baking sheet. Bake for 10 to 12 minutes. When cool, dip the tip of each cookie into melted chocolate and leave to harden on wire rack. Makes 5 dozen.

Piped Cookies
Spritsar

225 g (8 oz.) butter
1 dl (½ cup) sugar
1 egg yolk
1 teaspoon almond extract or 3 grated
 bitter amonds (optional)
¾ dl (⅓ cup) blanched almonds
4 ¾ dl (2 ¼ cups) sifted all-purpose flour
 (225 g)

Preheat oven to 175°C (350°F). Cream the butter and sugar until light and fluffy. Beat in the egg yolk and almond extract. Grind the almonds and add together with the flour. Work the dough until smooth and well blended. Press it through cookie press into long strips, cut them in 10 cm (4-inch) pieces. Shape into rings or S's and place on baking sheet. Bake for about 10 minutes. Makes 5 dozen.

How to make piped cookies fast and easy: attach the star plate to the cookie press and fill with dough. Press it into long parallel strips. Then cut the strips, all at once, into 10 cm (4-inch) pieces. Shape into rings or S's and place on baking sheet.

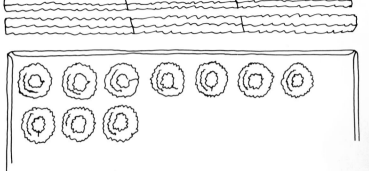

33

Piped Chocolate Cookies
Chokladspritsar

1 dl (½ cup) powdered sugar
1 tablespoon vanilla sugar
¾ dl (⅓ cup) cocoa
225 g (8 oz.) butter
1 egg yolk
4 ½ dl (2 cups) all-purpose flour (200 g)

In large mixing bowl, combine the sugar, vanilla sugar, cocoa, butter and egg yolk. Beat until creamy. Add the flour and work the dough till smooth and well blended. Chill for half an hour.

Preheat oven to 175°C (350°F). Press the dough through cookie press into long slender strips, cut them into 10 cm (4-inch) pieces. Shape each piece into a ring and place on baking sheet. Bake for about 10 minutes. When cool, sift with powdered sugar. Makes 5 dozen.

Piped Nut Cookies
Nötspritsar

225 g (8 oz.) butter
1 dl (½ cup) powdered sugar
½ tablespoon vanilla sugar
1 dl (½ cup) hazel nuts
4 ½ dl(2 cups) all-purpose flour (200 g)

Preheat oven to 175°C (350°F). Cream the butter and sugar together until light and fluffy. Grind the nuts and add together with the flour. Work the dough till smooth. Press it through cookie press into long narrow strips, cut them in 4-inch pieces. Shape into rings and place on baking sheet. Bake for about 10 minutes. Makes 5 dozen.

Sandbakelser or Almond Tarts
Mandelformar

175 g (6 oz.) butter *8 oz*
¾ dl (⅓ cup) sugar *- 1 C.*
1 egg ~~yolk~~
½ teaspoon almond extract (optional) *) ovr*
¾ dl (⅓ cup) blanched almonds *) vanilla*
3 dl (1 ½ cups) sifted all-purpose flour (150 g)
(2 C.)

Cream the butter and sugar, beat in the egg yolk and almond extract. Grind the almonds and add together with the flour; mix well. Chill the dough for 1 hour.

Preheat oven to 175°C (350°F). Divide the dough into 3 portions and shape into long logs. Cut each log in 12 pieces. Use your thumbs and press each piece into a buttered sandbakelse tin. Coat the bottom and the sides with an even layer of the dough.

Place the tins on baking sheet. Bake for 10 to 12 minutes or until light golden. Put the baking sheet on a wire rack and turn the tins upside down. Let cool for 3 to 4 minutes, then gently tap the bottom of each tin and remove. Makes 3 dozen.

Sandbakelser or Almond Tarts are delicious filled with whipped cream and fruit.

34

Dream Cookies
Drömmar

225 g (8 oz.) butter
2 dl (1 cup) sugar
2 teaspoons vanilla sugar
**5 ½ dl (2 ½ cups) sifted all-purpose flour
  (250 g)**
½ teaspoon ammonium carbonate

Preheat oven to 150°C (300°F). Cream the
butter, sugar and vanilla sugar till light
and fluffy. Add the flour mixed with
ammonium carbonate, blend well. Shape
the dough into small balls and place on
baking sheet. Bake for 20 to 25 minutes.
The cookies should be very pale and have
a cracked surface. Makes 5 dozen.

Place the tins on baking sheet. Bake for
10 to 12 minutes. Put the baking sheet on
a wire rack and turn the tins upside down.
Let cool for 3 to 4 minutes, then gently tap
the bottom of each tin and remove. Makes
2 dozen.

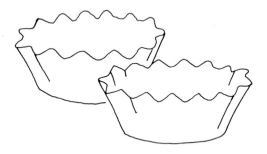

Oatmeal Tarts
Havreformar

100 g (4 oz.) butter
½ dl (¼ cup) sugar
1 dl (½ cup) oatmeal
2 dl (1 cup) sifted all-purpose flour (100 g)

In large mixing bowl, combine all the
ingredients. Work the dough with your
hands until well blended. Chill for 1 hour.
   Preheat oven to 175°C (350°F). Cut the
dough in half and shape into long logs.
Cut each log in 12 pieces. Use your
thumbs and press each piece into a buttered sandbakelse tin. Coat the bottom
and the sides with an even layer of the
dough.

Oatmeal Rusks
Havreskorpor

100 g (4 oz.) butter
1 dl (½ cup) sugar
1 egg *1 - 2*
2 dl (1 cup) sifted all-purpose flour (100 g)
2 ½ dl (1 cup) oatmeal
1 teaspoon baking powder
½ tablespoon ground cardamom

Preheat oven to 175°C (350°F). Cream the
butter and sugar. Beat in the eggs, one at a
time. Stir in the flour mixed with oatmeal,
baking powder and cardamom; blend
well.
   Drop the batter onto baking sheet in 2
strips about 4 cm (1 ½ inches) wide and

38 cm (15 inches) long. Bake for 15 to 20 minutes. Let cool for 5 minutes, then cut the strips in 2 ½ cm (1-inch) diagonal pieces. Spread them on the baking sheet and return to oven. Turn it off and leave the rusks to dry, about 2 hours. Makes 30.

Almond Rusks
Mandelskorpor
or Berlinerbröd

100 g (4 oz.) butter
1 dl (½ cup) sugar
2 eggs
1 dl (½ cup) coarsely chopped unblanched almonds
3 dl (1 ½ cups) sifted all-purpose flour (150 g)
1 teaspoon baking powder

Preheat oven to 175°C (350°F). Cream the butter and sugar. Beat in the eggs, one at a time. Stir in the almonds and the flour mixed with baking powder, blend well.

Drop the batter onto baking sheet in 3 strips, about 2 ½ cm (1 inch) wide and 30 cm (12 inches) long. Bake for 15 to 18 minutes. Let cool for 5 minutes, then cut the strips in 2 ½ cm (1-inch) diagonal pieces. Spread them on the baking sheet and return to oven. Turn it off and leave the rusks to dry, about 2 hours. Makes 3 dozen.

Coconut Rusks
Kokosskorpor

Follow the recipe for Almond Rusks substituting 2 dl (1 cup) flaked coconut for the almonds.

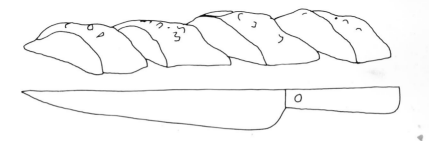

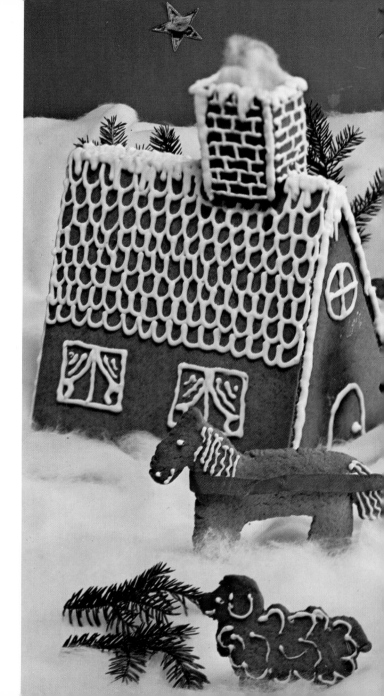

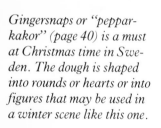

Gingersnaps or "peppar-kakor" (page 40) is a must at Christmas time in Sweden. The dough is shaped into rounds or hearts or into figures that may be used in a winter scene like this one.

Rolled Cookies

Rolled cookies take more time than most other cookies. However, the work is fun if the dough is thoroughly chilled, without being too hard, before you start rolling it out. Therefore, always put the cookie dough in a plastic bag and refrigerate for a couple of hours.

It is a good idea to roll the dough on a large baking sheet with nonstick finish: it is smooth, easy to clean and need not be floured. To prevent it from sliding, put a wet cloth between the baking sheet and the table top. If the dough has a tendency to stick to the rolling pin, flour it lightly. Should the dough become too soft and smeary before you have rolled it out, just pop the whole baking sheet into the refrigerator for 15 to 20 minutes, then continue rolling. Cut with cookie cutter and transfer the cookies to clean baking sheet. Gather the excess dough and roll it out again.

Swedish Gingersnaps
Pepparkakor

350 g (12 oz.) butter
4 ½ dl (2 cups) sugar
2 dl (1 cup) dark corn syrup
1 ½ tablespoons ginger
1 ½ tablespoons cardamom
1 ½ tablespoons cinnamon
1 tablespoon cloves
3 dl (1 ½ cups) whipping cream
1 tablespoon baking soda
19 dl (9 cups) sifted all-purpose flour
   (900 g)

Cream the butter together with sugar, syrup and spices. Add the cream whipped to a soft foam. Mix the baking soda with half of the flour and add to the batter. Gradually add the remaining flour. Turn the dough onto lightly floured surface and knead until smooth. Return the dough to the bowl, cover and refrigerate overnight.

Preheat oven to 200°C (400°F). Roll out part of the dough at a time directly on large baking sheet with nonstick finish. Roll the dough as thin as possible and cut with desired cookie cutters into rounds, hearts, stars, pigs or other figures. Remove excess dough from the baking sheet. Bake for 5 minutes, or until beautifully brown. Set the baking sheet on wire rack; remove the cookies when cool.

If desired, decorate the cookies with white frosting. Beat together 4 dl (2 cups) powdered sugar, 1 egg white and 1 teaspoon white vinegar. Fill an icing tube, or paper cone with fine opening, with the frosting and garnish the cookies. Or deco-

rate with blanched almonds before baking. Makes 300 to 400 gingersnaps.

Rye Rings
Rågringar

Cookies made with rye flour? It may seem
strange, but you will be surprised how
good they are.

225 g (8 oz.) butter
1 dl (½ cup) sugar
2 dl (1 cup) sifted rye flour (100 g)
3 ½ dl (1 ½ cups) sifted all-purpose flour
    (150 g)

Cream the butter and sugar. Add the two
kinds of flour and work the dough until
smooth. Chill for 2 hours.
    Preheat oven to 175°C (350°F). Roll out
the dough to ¼ cm (⅛-inch) thickness. Cut
with round 2-inch cookie cutter. Use the
cap from a small bottle and cut a hole in
each cookie a little off center. Prick the
cookies with a fork and place on baking
sheet. Bake for 8 to 10 minutes.
Makes 5 dozen.

Grandma's Jelly Cookies
Mormors syltkakor

1 quantity basic butter cookie dough,
    page 26
1 egg yolk

Garnish:
1 egg white, lightly beaten
2 tablespoons pearl sugar
2 tablespoons finely chopped
    unblanched almonds
2 tablespoons red currant jelly

Prepare the cookie dough adding the egg
yolk to the ingredients. Chill for 2 hours.
    Preheat oven to 175°C (350°F). Roll out
the dough to ¼ cm (⅛-inch) thickness. Cut
half the dough with round 5 cm (2-inch)
cookie cutter, place cookies on baking
sheet. Cut the remaining dough with scal-
loped 5 cm (2-inch) cookie cutter; cut a
hole in center of each cookie using the cap
from a small bottle. Brush the rings with
beaten egg white, dip them in pearl sugar
mixed with chopped almonds and place
on top of the round cookies. Fill the center
with jelly. Bake for 10 to 12 minutes.
Makes 30 cookies.

Lace Cookies

Lace cookies are shaped by draping over a round object such as a wooden spoon handle, a bottle or a roll of aluminium foil. If desired, serve the cookies brushed on the inside with melted chocolate. Remember that lace cookies are fragile and should be handled with great care.

The cookies may also be left to cool spread flat on wire rack; put them two and two together filled with butter cream or melted chocolate. Or stack them two or three on top of each other with whipped cream and fruit between the cookies.

Oatmeal Lace Cookies
Havreflarn

60 g (2 oz.) butter
2 dl (1 cup) oatmeal
1 ½ dl (⅔ cup) sugar
1 beaten egg
1 tablespoon flour
½ teaspoon baking powder

Preheat oven to 200°C (400°F). In small saucepan, melt the butter. Add the remaining ingredients, blend well. Drop the batter by small teaspoonfuls 4 inches apart on baking sheet, or into buttered platt pan. Bake for 4 to 8 minutes, or until the edges are light brown. Let cool for a minute or so, then hang the cookies over a bar to harden and finish cooling. To make thinner cookies, add ½ dl (¼ cup) whipping cream to the batter. Makes about 5 dozen.

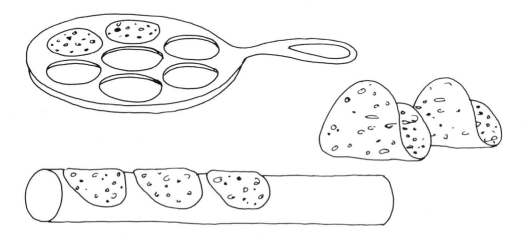

Strasbourg Cookies
Strassburgare

225 g (8 oz.) butter
1 dl (½ cup) powdered sugar
2 tablespoons vanilla sugar
2 dl (1 cup) sifted all-purpose flour (100 g)
2 dl (1 cup) potato starch flour

Preheat oven to 175°C (350°F). Cream the butter, sugar and vanilla sugar. Add the two kinds of flour (spoon the potato starch flour into the measuring cup) a little at a time, beating at high speed.

Press the dough through a no. 5 pastry tube into small flat roses or sticks directly onto cookie sheet. Bake for 10 minutes or until a pale golden. Makes 4 dozen.

If desired, sift with powdered sugar before serving. Or put the cookies together two and two with melted chocolate or firm strawberry jam between, then sift with powdered sugar.

Currant Cookies
Korintkakor

¾ dl (⅓ cup) currants
½ dl (¼ cup) cognac
100 g (4 oz.) butter
¾ dl (⅓ cup) sugar
1 egg
4 ½ dl (2 cups) sifted all-purpose flour (200 g)
1 teaspoon baking powder

Preheat oven to 175°C (350°F). In a small cup, combine the currants and cognac; leave to soak for 15 minutes.

Cream the butter and sugar, add the egg and stir vigorously. Blend in the currants and cognac, then add the flour mixed with baking powder. Blend well by hand. Drop the batter by tablespoonfuls onto baking sheet. Bake for 10 to 12 minutes. Let cool spread on wire rack. Makes 30 cookies.

Anna's Almond Cookies
Annas mandelkakor

225 g (8 oz.) almond paste
2 egg whites, lightly beaten

Garnish
candied orange peel

Preheat oven to 175°C (350°F). Grate the
almond paste on the coarse side of the
grater. Combine with the egg whites and
work until smooth and free from lumps.
Drop the batter in small mounds onto
baking sheet. Press a sliver of candied
orange peel into each cookie.

Bake for 8 to 10 minutes. The cookies
will turn light golden and become firm on
the surface; the inside will remain soft and
chewy. To retain their moisture, store the
cookies in a tight container together with a
slice of white bread. Makes 20 cookies.

Coconut Cookies
Kokoskakor

2 eggs
1 dl (½ cup) sugar
9 dl (4 cups) flaked coconut
50 g (2 oz.) butter, melted

Preheat oven to 175°C (350°F). Beat the
eggs and sugar till white and fluffy. Add
the coconut and butter, blend well. Drop
the batter by tablespoonfuls onto baking
sheet. Bake for 12 to 15 minutes. Makes
3 dozen.

To retain their moisture, store the
cookies in a tight container together with a
slice of white bread.

Pastries

*K*affe med bakelser, coffee with pastries. Swedes can be seen indulging in this favorite pastime any time of the day: midmorning, noon, midafternoon and evening.

Konditori or *kafé* is the name for the Swedish coffee house which often has an old-fashioned interior with comfortable chairs, little round tables, potted plants and small lamps spreading a soft light. The konditori is an almost sacred place to the Swede; it is well suited for an hour of contemplation, or for a quiet talk with your friend. Indeed, many Swedish pastry-loving poets have confessed their love of the konditori atmosphere and find it a good place to work in.

After exhaustive shopping in town, it is heaven to sink down in the konditori sofa and have a stimulating cup of coffee and a creamy pastry.

It is most difficult to resist the Swedish konditori counter display. Its array of delicious *bakelser* – cream puffs, macaroons, rich bars and cupcakes – is designed to melt your will power and make you forget all about your diet.

Here you will learn how to prepare some of the most popular Swedish pastries.

Basic Pastry Dough

Many *bakelser* call for a shell or bottom crust made from this pastry.

100 g (4 oz.) butter
¾ dl (⅓ cup) sugar
1 egg yolk
2 ½ dl (1 ⅓ cups) sifted all-purpose flour
(135 g)

Cream the butter and sugar. Stir in the egg yolk. Add the flour and work the dough with your hands until well blended and smooth.

Mazarins
Mazariner

The mazarin is the number one Swedish pastry.

Shells
1 quantity basic pastry dough

Filling
100 g (4 oz.) butter
½ dl (¼ cup sugar
225 g (8 oz.) almond paste
3 eggs
½ dl (¼ cup) sifted all-purpose flour (25 g)

Frosting
2 dl (1 cup) powdered sugar
about 2 tablespoons water

Preheat oven to 175°C (350°F). Prepare the pastry dough. Shape the dough into a long log and cut in 18 pieces. Press each piece into a buttered muffin tin to coat the bottom and the side.

To make the filling, beat together the butter, sugar and almond paste. When creamy and free from lumps, beat in the eggs one at a time.

Stir in the flour. Blend well. Spoon the filling into the lined muffin tins. Bake for 20 to 25 minutes, or until golden. Let cool for 5 minutes and gently unmold.

Stir the powdered sugar with water to make a thin glaze; spread on top of the pastries while still slightly warm. Or simply sift with powdered sugar. Serve the mazarins warm or at room temperature. Makes 18.

The most beloved Swedish pastry may be the almond-flavored Mazarin.

Tosca Bars
Toscabitar

Crust
1 quantity basic pastry dough, page 46

Filling
100 g (4 oz.) butter
½ dl (¼ cup) sugar
225 g (8 oz.) almond paste
3 eggs
¾ dl (⅓ cup) sifted all-purpose flour (35 g)
1 teaspoon baking powder

Topping
100 g (4 oz.) butter
1 dl (½ cup) sugar
2 dl (1 cup) sliced almonds
2 tablespoons flour
2 tablespoons milk

Preheat oven to 175°C (350°F). Prepare
the pastry dough. Press it out on the bottom of a buttered cake pan, 25 by 30 cm
(10 by 12 inches).

Beat together the butter, sugar and
almond paste. When smooth and creamy,
beat in the eggs, one at a time. Blend in
the flour mixed with baking powder.
Spread the filling on top of the pastry.
Bake for 15 to 20 minutes.

To make the topping, melt the butter in
small saucepan. Add the remaining ingredients and bring to a simmer stirring constantly. Do not boil! Remove from heat.

When the cake is done, spread it with
the warm topping. Switch from "bake" to
"broil" and return the cake to the oven.
Broil until golden brown. Let the cake
cool in the pan. Cut in bars 4 by 6 cm
(1½ by 2½ inches). Makes 30.

If you like, brush the bottom and the
sides of each bar with melted chocolate.

Orange Pastries
Apelsinsnitt

Crust
1 quantity basic pastry dough, page 46

Filling
225 g (8 oz.) almond paste
¾ dl (⅓ cup) powdered sugar
grated rind of 1 orange
1 egg white

Frosting
2 dl (1 cup) powdered sugar
about 2 tablespoons fresh orange juice

Garnish
½ dl (¼ cup) finely chopped candied
  orange peel

Preheat oven to 175°C (350°F). Prepare
the pastry dough. If too soft to handle,
chill for 30 minutes. Roll the dough into a
rectangle, 12 by 35 cm (5 by 14 inches).

Beat together the almond paste, sugar,
grated orange rind and egg white until
well blended and smooth. Shape into a 35
cm (14-inch) log and place on top of the
pastry. Wrap the dough around the log
and place it, seam-side down, on baking
sheet. Bake for 18 to 20 minutes.

Stir the powdered sugar with orange
juice to a thin glaze; frost the roll while
still warm. Before the frosting hardens,
sprinkle with chopped orange peel. Let
cool, then cut in 1-inch pieces. Makes 14.

Platt Pastries
Plättbakelser

100 g (4 oz.) butter
¾ dl (⅓ cup) sugar
2 eggs
**1 ½ dl (⅔ cup) sifted all-purpose flour
  (70 g)**

Garnish
**2 tablespoons chopped unblanched
  almonds**
2 tablespoons pearl sugar

Preheat oven to 200°C (400°F). Cream the
butter and sugar. Beat in the eggs, one at a
time. Blend in the flour. Butter a platt pan
and spread 2 teaspoons of the batter in each
round. Sprinkle with chopped almonds
mixed with pearl sugar. Bake for 8 to 10
minutes, or until golden.

  Remove the cakes and hang them over a
bottle, wooden spoon handle or rolling pin.
Remove the pastries when cool and crisp.

  Butter the platt pan again and continue
baking. Always let the pan cool before
spreading the batter. Makes 28.

Half-Moons
Halvmånar

1 quantity platt pastries

Filling
apple sauce
or apricot marmalade
or red currant jelly

Frosting
2 dl (1 cup) powdered sugar
about 2 tablespoons water

Garnish
**2 tablespoons chopped pistachio nuts
  or citron**
**2 tablespoons chopped candied orange
  peel**

Bake the platt pastries omitting the garnish. Let the cakes cool flat on wire rack.
Put them together in pairs with desired
filling.

  Frost the pastries with powdered sugar
stirred with water to a thin glaze. Before
the frosting hardens, sprinkle with chopped nuts and orange peel. Cut into half-
moons. Makes 28.

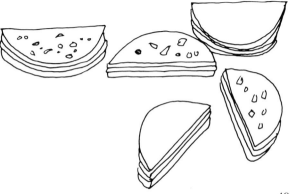

Almond Wafers
Äkta mandelspån

These elegant, old-fashioned almond wafers are sometimes served at weddings and other very festive occasions. If you do not have the special wafer rack, use a thick cardboard roll (the size of a rolling pin) wrapped in aluminium foil.

225 g (8 oz.) almond paste
2 dl (1 cup) powdered sugar
1 egg white
1 sheet wafer (rice) paper 23 by 27 cm
(9 by 11 inches)

Frosting
1 cup powdered sugar
about 2 tablespoons water

Garnish
½ dl (¼ cup) finely chopped candied
orange peel
½ dl (¼ cup) finely chopped citron
15 chopped pistachio nuts

Preheat oven to 200°C (400°F). Beat the almond paste together with sugar and egg white until smooth. Spread the batter gently onto the wafer paper in a smooth, even layer. Cut the sheet with scissors into 3 strips lengthwise, then cut each strip across in 12 pieces. Lay them on buttered wafer rack. Bake until light golden, about 6 minutes. Let the wafers cool on the rack.

Stir the powdered sugar with water to a thin glaze. Frost the wafers on top and, before the frosting hardens, sprinkle with chopped fruit and nuts. These wafers are crisp on the outside and chewy inside; store them in a tight container. Serve with ice cream, fruit compote, tea or coffee. If desired, arrange them in the shape of a pyramid; sticking together with melted sugar. Makes 3 dozen.

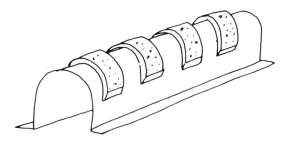

Basic Puff Pastry
Enkel smördeg

225 g (8 oz.) butter
**4 dl (2 cups) sifted all-purpose flour
  (200 g)**
¾ dl (⅓ cup) cold water

In large mixing bowl, rapidly rub the butter into the flour between the tips of your fingers. When crumbly, pour in the cold water. Quickly gather the crumbs and knead into a rough ball. Cover and chill 1 hour.

Roll the dough into a 30 cm (12-inch) square. Fold in 3 like a cloth, then in 3 again so that you have a small, square package. Put the dough in plastic bag and chill for 2 hours.

Butter Rings
Smörkransar

1 quantity basic puff pastry

Garnish
1 beaten egg
pearl sugar

Prepare the pastry; roll, fold and refrigerate. Roll it out to ½ cm (¼-inch) thickness. Cut with ring-shaped 5 cm (2-inch) cookie cutter. Or use a round 5 cm (2-inch) cookie cutter, then use the cap from a small bottle and cut a hole in center of each cookie.

Lay the rings on baking sheet, cover and set aside for 30 minutes.

Preheat oven to 225°C (450°F). Brush the top of each ring with beaten egg and dip in pearl sugar. Bake for 7 to 9 minutes, or until risen and golden. Let cool on wire rack. Makes 3 dozen.

French Waffles
Franska våfflor

1 quantity basic puff pastry

Butter cream filling
100 g (4 oz.) butter
2 dl (1 cup) powdered sugar
1 egg yolk
**½ tablespoon Swedish punch or vanilla
  sugar**

Prepare the pastry; roll, fold and refrigerate. Roll the dough into a 30 cm (12-inch) square. Cut with round 5 cm (2-inch) cookie cutter. Use a small, knobbed rolling pin and roll each circle on both sides in sugar into an oval cookie about 6 cm (2 ½ inches) across and 15 cm (6 inches) long. Lay them on baking sheet, cover and set aside for 30 minutes.

Preheat oven to 225°C (450°F). Bake for 5 to 6 minutes, or until light golden. Let cool on wire rack.

Cream the butter and sugar until white and fluffy. Beat in the egg yolk. Flavor to taste with punch or vanilla. Put the cookies together in pairs with the filling between. Makes 20.

Rosettes
Struvor

These thin-walled, sugar-dipped, exceedingly tender pastries may take the shape of a star, a flower or a butterfly, depending on the type of rosette iron used.

1 egg
2 dl (1 cup) milk
½ dl (¼ cup) light beer
½ tablespoon sugar
2 dl (1 cup) sifted all-purpose flour (100 g)

For cooking
vegetable shortening

Garnish
sugar

Beat together the egg, milk, beer, sugar and flour to a smooth batter. Pour into a small bowl, cover and refrigerate for 1 hour.

Heat the fat in small, heavy-bottomed pan to 175°C (350°F). If you do not have a fat thermometer, test the temperature with a piece of white bread; it should brown just before you have counted to 60.

Heat the rosette iron in the fat until really hot. Stir the batter. Wipe the hot iron quickly with paper towel and dip to ¾ into the batter. Lower the iron into the fat and cook the rosette till golden brown, about 1 minute. Carefully remove the rosette with help of a fork and place on wire rack lined with paper towels. Let cool for 1 minute, then dip the rosette in sugar.

Continue cooking the pastries. As soon as the rosette is cooked and removed, dip the hot iron into the fat. Stir the batter now and then. Makes 3 dozen.

Curlicues
Krumelurer

7 eggs whites
1 egg yolk
1 ½ dl (¾ cup) sugar
2 dl (1 cup) sifted all-purpose flour (200 g)

For cooking
oil or vegetable shortening

Beat together 4 egg whites, egg yolk and sugar. Stir in the flour. Beat the remaining egg whites into stiff peak, and turn into the batter.

Heat the fat in a heavy-bottomed pan to 180°C (350°F). If you do not have a fat thermometer, test the temperature with a piece of white bread; it should brown just before you have counted to 60.

Fill a funnel with batter. Make a pastry by coiling 1 tablespoon of batter into the hot fat. Let cook until golden brown, about 1 minute.

Remove the pastry from the fat and let it drain on a paper towel. Makes about 35 pastries.

Curlicues, Rosettes and Krumkaker. The recipe for Krumkaker, page 56.

Christmas Stars
Julstjärnor

1 quantity basic puff pastry, page 51

Filling
16 pitted prunes

Garnish
1 beaten egg

Prepare the pastry; roll, fold and refrigerate. Roll it out to a 30 cm (12-inch) square. Cut in 7 cm (3-inch) squares and put a pitted prune in center of each. Cut a 3 ½ cm (1 ½-inch) slit in each corner and fold every other point toward center; press the points together. Place on baking sheet, cover and set aside for 30 minutes.

Preheat oven to 225°C (450°F). Paint the top of each pastry with beaten egg. Bake for 8 to 10 minutes, or until risen and golden. Let cool on wire rack. Makes 16.

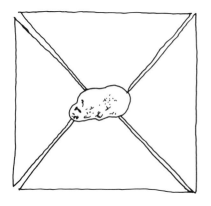

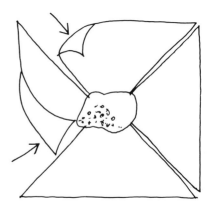

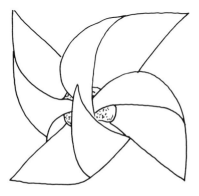

Crullers
Klenäter

In Sweden these pastries are called *klenä-ter*, in Norway *fattigmann*.

4 egg yolks
½ dl (¼ cup) sugar
¼ teaspoon salt
1 tablespoon akvavit or cognac
grated rind of 1 lemon
2 tablespoons softened butter
2 dl (1 cup) sifted all-purpose flour
   (100 g)

For cooking
vegetable shortening

Garnish
sugar

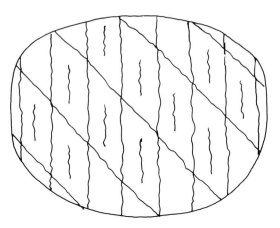

Stir together the egg yolks, sugar, salt, akvavit and lemon rind. Add the butter and flour; quickly work the dough together. Chill for 2 hours.

Roll out the dough on lightly floured surface to little more than ¼ cm (⅛-inch) thickness. Use a ruler and cut the dough with pastry wheel into slanted strips, 2 ½ by 10 cm (1 by 4 inches). Cut a 2½ cm (1-inch) slit in center of each strip and pull one end through the slit.

Heat the fat in heavy-bottomed pan to 175°C (350°F). The fat should be about 7 cm (3 inches) deep. Cook a few crullers at a time until golden, about 1 minute. Drain on paper towel for a minute, then dip both sides in sugar. Makes about 30.

Ambrosia Pastries
Ambrosiabakelser

Cake
6 eggs
4 dl (2 cups) sugar
350 g (12 oz.) butter, melted
**4 ½ dl (2 cups) sifted all-purpose flour
   (200 g)**

For moistening the cake
1 dl (½ cup) rum

Frosting
4 dl (2 cups) powdered sugar
3 to 4 tablespoons fresh orange juice

Garnish
**1 dl (½ cup) finely chopped candied
   orange peel**

Preheat oven to 175°C (375°F). Butter a
sheet cake pan, 27 by 40 cm (11 by 16
inches), and sprinkle it with bread
crumbs.

Beat the eggs and sugar till thick and
pale. Add the melted butter and flour,
blend well. Pour the batter into the pan.
Bake for 15 to 18 minutes. Set the pan on a
wire rack and leave the cake to cool
covered with a cloth.

Sprinkle the cake with the rum. Stir the
powdered sugar with orange juice to a thin
glaze and frost the cake, then sprinkle
with chopped orange peel. Cut the cake
into 4 long strips, then cut each strip into
12 triangles. Makes 4 dozen.

Maria Puffs
Mariabollar, Tebollar

Here is an old-fashioned cream puff with a
cracked crust.

Crust
½ quantity basic pastry dough, page 46

Cream puff paste
2 ¼ dl)1 cup) water
100 g (4 oz.) butter, cut in pieces
2 dl (1 cup) sifted all-purpose flour (100 g)
4 eggs

Filling
3 dl (1 ½ cups) whipping cream
***or* 3 quantities vanilla custard filling,
   page 82**

Preheat oven to 175°C (375°F). Prepare
the pastry dough; shape into an 8-inch
log, chill 1 hour.

In a saucepan, combine the water and
butter. Bring to a boil and let cook over
low heat until the butter has melted. Add
the flour all at once and beat vigorously
with a wooden spoon for 2 minutes or till
the batter leaves the side of the pan.
Remove from heat, let cool for a couple of
minutes. Beat in the eggs, one at a time.
When the last egg has been absorbed by
the batter, beat for 2 minutes more.

Drop the batter by large tablespoonfuls
5 cm (2 inches) apart on baking sheet. Cut
the chilled pastry in ½ cm (¼-inch) slices
and place on top of each batter mound.

Bake for about 30 minutes, or until the
puffs are golden brown, crusty and doubled in size. Cut the puffs in two horizon-

tally; with a fork remove any uncooked portions. Let the halves cool on rack, then fill with whipped cream or vanilla custard. Dust top with powdered sugar, serve at once. Makes 16.

Krumkaker
Tunnrån, Gorån

In Scandinavian communities in the United States these pastries are best known by their Norwegian name, *krum-kaker*. To make them you need a special krumkake iron.

3 eggs
1 dl (½ cup) sugar
100 g (4 oz.) butter, melted
1 ¾ dl (¾ cup) sifted all-purpose flour (75 g)
½ teaspoon ground cardamom

Beat the eggs and sugar until thick. Stir in the melted butter and flour mixed with cardamom. Blend well.

Heat the krumkake iron on both sides over moderate heat. Brush with butter and put about ½ tablespoon batter in center of the iron. Close it and bake for a minute on both sides, or until golden. Roll the cake quickly into a "cigar" and let cool on wire rack. Makes 20. (See photo on page 53.)

Almond Chocolate Pastries
Chokladfyllda mandelflarn

100 g (4 oz.) butter
2 dl (1 cup) chopped blanched almonds
1 dl (½ cup) sugar
2 tablespoons flour
3 tablespoons milk

Filling
1 dl (½ cup) semi-sweet chocolate morsels, melted

Preheat oven to 200°C (400°F). In a small saucepan, melt the butter. Add the almonds, sugar, flour and milk; bring to a simmer on low heat stirring constantly. Remove from heat.

Drop the batter by small teaspoonfuls into each depression on a buttered platt pan or 10 cm (4 inches) apart on cookie sheet. Bake for 7 to 8 minutes or until light brown. Allow to cool for 1 minute, then remove the cookies and finish cooling on wire rack. Sandwich the cookies in pairs with melted chocolate between. Makes 18.

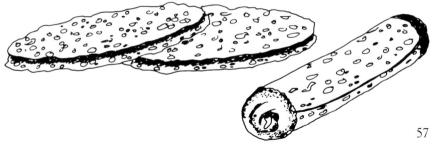

Basic Cake for Pastries

Some of the nicest and simplest Swedish pastries are made of light sponge cake.

3 eggs
1 dl (½ cup) sugar
1 ½ dl (⅔ cup) sifted cake or all-purpose flour (60 g)
1 teaspoon baking powder

Preheat oven to 225°C (425°F). Beat the eggs and sugar until thick and pale. Mix the flour and baking powder, stir into the egg batter. Blend well. Spread the batter in a sheet cake pan, 27 by 40 cm (11 by 16 inches), that has been lined with buttered aluminum foil. Bake for about 5 minutes or until golden. Place the pan on wire rack and let the cake cool covered with a cloth.

Strawberry Pastries
Jordgubbsbakelser

Spread the cake with vanilla custard filling (see page 82) and roll up from the long side. Cut in 4 cm (1 ½-inch) slices. Cover each slice with a dab of whipped cream and decorate with fresh strawberries.

Mandarin Pastries
Mandarinbakelser

Cut the cake in two strips and sandwich them with orange-flavored whipped cream between and on top. Beat 2 dl (1 cup) whipping cream until stiff and blend with ½ dl (¼ cup) frozen concentrated orange juice. Cut the cake in bars 5 by 7 cm (2 by 3 inches). Garnish each pastry with a row of drained mandarin oranges. Chill before serving.

Princess Pastries
Prinsessbakelser

Cut the cake with round 5 cm (2-inch) cookie cutter. Sandwich the cakes in pairs with vanilla custard filling between (see page 82). Prepare marzipan (see directions on the can of almond paste) and color a light green. Roll out the marzipan to ¼ cm (⅛-inch) thickness and cut in strips 1 cm (½-inch) wider than the height of the cakes. Wrap the cakes with the marzipan and fill the top with whipped cream. Decorate with grapes or mandarin oranges.

Potato Pastries
Potatisbakelser

Cut the cake with round 5 cm (2-inch) cookie cutter. Sandwich the cakes two and two with vanilla custard (page 82) or apple sauce between. Cover each pastry with a circle of marzipan, tuck it in under the pastry. Sift with cocoa and place in a fluted paper cup.

Congress Pastries
Kongresser

Shells
100 g (4 oz.) butter
2 dl (1 cup) sifted all-purpose flour (100 g)
2 tablespoons cold water

Filling
2 dl (1 cup) hazelnuts or blanched almonds
2 eggs
1 dl (½ cup) sugar

Rub the butter into the flour. When crumbly, add the water and work quickly into a rough ball. Cover the bowl and chill for 2 hours.

Grind the nuts or chop them finely. Beat the eggs and sugar together until pale and fluffy, blend in the nuts.

Shape ⅔ of the chilled dough into a log and cut in 12 pieces. Coat the inside of 12 buttered muffin tins with the dough and fill with the nut batter. Roll out the remaining dough and cut with pastry wheel into thin strips. Place the strips crosswise on top of the pastries. Bake for 20 to 25 minutes in a 175°C (350°F) oven. Let cool for a few minutes and gently unmold the pastries. Makes 12 pastries.

Small sandbakelse tins are often used for this kind of pastries; the recipe yields 24 such mini pastries.

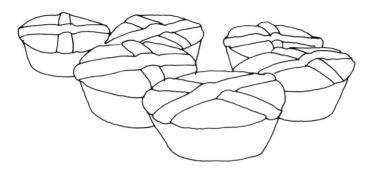

Vanilla Hearts
Vaniljhjärtan

Heart-shaped tartlet tins are commonly used for these pastries but also boat-shaped tins or sandbakelse tins may be used.

Shells
1 quantity basic pastry dough, page 46

Vanilla custard filling
2 dl (1 cup) light cream
2 egg yolks
1 tablespoon sugar
2 teaspoons corn starch
1 tablespoon vanilla sugar

Garnish
powdered sugar

Preheat oven to 175°C (350°F). Prepare the pastry dough and set aside.

In a saucepan, combine the cream, egg yolks, sugar and corn starch. (Do not use an aluminum pan unless it has the non-stick finish or the custard will turn light green.) Bring to a simmer continuously stirring and cook until thickened. Let cool covered and stir in the vanilla.

Cut the pastry dough in two. Shape one part into a log and cut in 12 pieces; press each piece into a buttered tartlet tin. Fill the tins with the custard. Roll out the remaining dough to ¼ cm (⅛-inch) thickness and cover the tins with a lid of the dough.

Place the tins on cookie sheet and bake for 15 to 18 minutes or until light brown. Wait for a few minutes and gently unmold the pastries. Let cool uncovered on cookie sheet. Turn the pastries lid-side up and sift with powdered sugar. Serve newly baked. Makes 12 pastries.

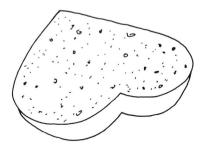

Heartshaped tartlets with vanilla custard filling are very, very good.

60

Filled Pastry Cones
Fyllda strutar

Cones
50 g (2 oz.) butter
½ dl (¼ cup) sugar
½ tablespoon vanilla sugar
1 egg
1 dl (½ cup) sifted all-purpose flour (50 g)

Filling
3 dl (1 ½ cups) whipping cream
4 dl (2 cups) fresh strawberries

Preheat oven to 200°C (400°F). Cream the butter, sugar and vanilla. Add the egg beating at high speed. Stir in the flour, blend well.

Drop the batter by large tablespoonfuls onto a teflon baking sheet (baking sheet without nonstick finish must first be buttered and floured). Use the back of a teaspoon and spread the batter into 15 cm (6-inch) circles. Bake for 3 to 4 minutes, or till the edges turn light brown. Use a spatula and turn each circle around, then quickly shape into a cone and place in a bottle to cool and stiffen. Should the cakes get too cool and crisp to shape, return to oven for a minute. Do not bake more than 3 cones at a time. You will get 8 cones in all.

Whip the cream thick. Slice the strawberries, saving 8 good-looking berries, and fold into the cream. Add sugar if desired. Fill the cones immediately before serving: spoon the cream and berry mixture into the cones and top with a whole berry. Stand the cones in a glass bowl filled with marbles and bring to the table, or put each cone on a plate. Serve with a fork. Makes 8 servings.

Instead of strawberries, any kind of fresh or frozen berries may be used.

Mix the whipped cream with 1 ½ dl (⅔ cup) lingonberry or cranberry preserve and you will have an old Swedish dessert called *Giftas* or "Married".

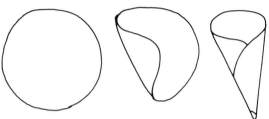

Crisp Waffles
Frasvåfflor

4 dl (2 cups) whipping cream
3 dl (1 ½ cups) sifted all-purpose flour (150 g)
1 dl (½ cup) ice cold water
2 tablespoons melted butter
1 tablespoon sugar

Beat the cream until fluffy. Combine the flour, water and part of the cream; beat until smooth. Fold in remaining cream, butter and sugar. Let batter stand in refrigerator 1 hour.

Heat the waffle iron and brush with butter. Cook waffles on hot, but not too hot iron. It is not necessary to brush with butter between each waffle. Place waffles on rack or, if possible, serve directly with jam and whipped cream or vanilla ice cream. 4 to 5 servings.

Sponge Cakes

S wedish cakes are often baked in a cast iron skillet, ideal for even baking. Old and well used skillets need only be buttered, the same goes for cake pans with nonstick finish. New skillets and aluminum pans without the special finish must be buttered and floured, or, as is common in Sweden, sprinkled with fine dry bread crumbs. The crumbs give a nice crust to the cake.

Bread crumbs may be bought ready-made or you can prepare them yourself: spread slices of stale white bread on baking sheet and put in a 150°C (300°F) oven until thoroughly dry. Break the bread into an electric blender and whirl till pulverized. Or put the bread in a plastic bag and roll with a rolling pin.

Always bake the cake in the middle third of the oven. It is done when a toothpick inserted in center comes out clean; at the same time the cake starts to shrink from the sides of the pan and springs back to a light touch of the finger.

Let the cake cool for two minutes in the pan before inverting it onto a wire rack. Let cool covered with a cloth. Wash the cake pan and wipe it dry. Transfer the cake to a platter and store it covered with the pan.

Sponge-cake flavored with vanilla or lemon is a very common and popular treat with coffee in Sweden (page 66).

Light Sponge Cake
Sockerkaka

The most popular cake in Sweden? The *sockerkaka*, of course. It is usually flavored with vanilla or grated lemon rind.

3 eggs
2 dl (1 cup) sugar
grated rind of 1 lemon
or 1 tablespoon vanilla sugar
2 ½ dl (1 ⅓ cups) sifted all-purpose flour
(135 g)
2 teaspoons baking powder
100 g (4 oz.) butter, melted
¾ dl (⅓ cup) warm water

Preheat oven to 175°C (350°F). Butter a 1 ½ liter (6-cup) ring mold or bread pan and sprinkle it with bread crumbs.

Beat the eggs and sugar till thick and pale. Add the desired flavoring. Mix the flour and baking powder, stir into the batter together with melted butter. Add the water and blend well.

Pour the batter into the pan. Bake for 40 to 45 minutes, or till a toothpick inserted in center comes out clean.

Cinnamon Cake
Kanelkaka

Follow the recipe for light sponge-cake, omitting the vanilla or lemon rind. Add instead 1 tablespoon cinnamon mixed in with the flour.

Spice Cake
Pepparkaka

Follow the recipe for light sponge-cake, omitting the vanilla or lemon rind. Add instead 1 teaspoon cloves and ½ tablespoon each of cardamom, cinnamon and ginger mixed in with the flour.

Chocolate Cake
Chokladkaka

Follow the recipe for light sponge-cake; flavor the batter with vanilla. Add 3 tablespoons cocoa mixed in with the flour.

Apple Cupcakes
Äppelmuffins

The light sponge-cake batter may also be used for making cupcakes, in Sweden called *muffins*. Makes approximately 18 cupcakes.

Follow the recipe for light sponge-cake, flavor the batter with grated lemon rind. Fill paper-lined muffin tins to ⅔ with batter. Peel and cut 2 apples in wedges, dip them in sugar mixed with cinnamon. Stick a wedge into each muffin tin. Bake for about 15 minutes.

Raisin Cupcakes
Russinmuffins

Follow the recipe for light sponge-cake;
flavor the batter with grated lemon rind.
Add 1 dl (½ cup) raisins mixed with the
flour. Fill paper-lined muffin tins to ⅔
with batter. Bake for about 15 minutes.

Orange Cupcakes
Apelsinmuffins

Follow the recipe for light sponge-cake;
flavor the batter with grated orange rind
instead of lemon rind. Fill paper-lined
muffin tins to ⅔ with batter. Bake for
about 15 minutes. If desired, frost the
cupcakes with 1 dl (1 cup) powdered
sugar stirred with 2 tablespoons orange
juice.

Cinnamon Apple Cake
Kaneläppelkaka

4 eggs
2 dl (1 cup) sugar
225 g (8 oz.) butter
3 dl (1 ½ cups) sifted all-purpose flour
   (150 g)
1 teaspoon baking powder
3 apples
½ dl (¼ cup) sugar
2 teaspoons cinnamon

Preheat oven to 175°C (350°F). Butter a
25 cm (10-inch) cast iron skillet or cake
pan, then sprinkle with fine dry bread
crumbs.

Beat the eggs and sugar till thick and
pale. Add the melted butter and flour
mixed with baking powder, blend well.
Pour the batter into the skillet. Peel and
cut the apples in wedges, dip in the sugar
mixed with cinnamon. Stick the apples
into the cake batter. Bake for 30 to 35
minutes. Serve the cake hot or at room
temperature.

Sultan Cake
Sultankaka

This is the traditional Swedish fruit cake.

2 dl (1 cup) raisins
1 dl (½ cup) chopped candied orange peel
1 dl (½ cup) chopped candied citron
1 dl (½ cup) chopped almonds
2 dl (1 cup) sifted all-purpose flour
3 egg whites
225 g (8 oz.) butter
1 ½ dl (⅔ cup) sugar
3 egg yolks

Preheat oven to 175°C (350°F). Butter a 1 ½ liter (6-cup) bread pan. Sprinkle it with bread crumbs.

Stir together the fruit, almonds and flour. Drop the egg whites into clean mixing bowl and beat until they form stiff peaks. In large mixing bowl, cream the butter and sugar till light and fluffy. Beat in the egg yolks one at a time. Stir in the flour mixture, then fold in the beaten egg whites.

Pour the batter into the pan. Cover with aluminum foil. Bake for 30 minutes, then remove the foil without moving the pan. Bake for another 30 minutes, or until done. Wait for 3 to 4 days before serving the cake.

Cardamom Cake
Kardemummakaka

6 eggs
3 dl (1 ⅓ cups) sugar
9 dl (4 cups) sifted all-purpose flour (400 g)
1 tablespoon baking powder
1 ½ tablespoons ground cardamom
4 dl (2 cups) milk
225 g (8 oz.) butter, melted

Preheat oven to 175°C (350°F). Butter a heavy 2 ½ liter (12-cup) bundt pan or a similar large ring mold. Sprinkle it, if necessary, with bread crumbs.

Beat the eggs and sugar till thick and pale. Mix the flour, baking powder and cardamom, stir into the egg batter. Add the milk and melted butter, blend well. Pour the batter into the pan. Bake for about 50 minutes.

If you don't have a large ring mold, use two smaller ones or use two bread pans. The baking time will then be about 35 minutes.

The rich, classical fruit cake called "Sultankaka" contains raisins, chopped candied fruit and almonds.

Lingon Cake
Lingonkaka

5 eggs
2 ½ dl (1 ¼ cups) sugar
225 g (8 oz.) butter, melted
2 dl (1 cup) lingonberry (or cranberry)
  preserves
1 dl (½ cup) sour cream
5 ½ dl (2 ½ cups) sifted all-purpose flour
  (250 g)
1 tablespoon cinnamon
1 tablespoon ginger
1 teaspoon cloves
1 tablespoon baking soda

Preheat oven to 175°C (350°F). Butter a
heavy 2 ½ liter (12-cup) bundt pan or similar large ring mold. Sprinkle it, if necessary, with bread crumbs.

In large mixing bowl, beat the eggs and
sugar till thick and pale. Stir in the butter,
lingonberries or cranberries and sour
cream. Add the flour mixed with spices
and baking soda, blend well.

Pour the batter into the pan. Bake for
40 minutes or till a toothpick inserted in
center comes out clean.

If you don't have a large ring mold, use
two smaller ones or use two bread pans.
The baking time will then be about 30
minutes.

Party Cakes

A *tårta* is a fancy party cake that is filled and frosted. At a festive coffee party, the tårta is served last; after the buns, cakes and cookies are carefully enjoyed you are supposed to manage at least a small piece of rich tårta.

Most common and very popular is the *grädd-tårta* or cream cake – layers of light sponge cake are layered with fruit and covered with whipped cream – but there are many other classic Swedish tårtas some of which are presented here.

Assemble the cream cake directly on the serving plate; protect the plate by putting four strips of waxed paper under the sides of the cake. When frosted and ready to serve, remove the strips. Today, cream cakes are usually garnished in a very simple way: whipped cream is just spread with a spatula over the top and the sides of the cake.

Basic Cake
Tårtbotten

4 eggs
2 dl (1 cup) sugar
2 dl (1 cup) sifted all-purpose flour (100 g)

Preheat oven to 200°C (400°F). Butter and flour three 23 cm (9-inch) cake pans.

Beat the eggs and sugar until pale and thick. Stir in the flour, mix well. Divide the batter in the cake pans. Bake for 7 to 9 minutes. Invert the cakes onto a wire rack lined with waxed paper. Let cool covered with a terry towel.

Cream Cake
Gräddtårta

1 quantity basic cake

Filling
4 dl (2 cups) fresh, canned or frozen fruit, any kind,
or **apple sauce**
or **strawberry jam**
or **vanilla custard filling, page 82**

Garnish
4 dl (2 cups) whipping cream
fresh or canned fruit

Assemble the cake with any of the suggested fillings between the layers. Whip the cream stiff, add sugar if desired. Cover the top and the sides of the cake with cream. Garnish with fruit, e.g. sliced peaches, grapes or fresh berries. Chill well before serving.

Strawberry Cake
Jordgubbstårta

1 quantity basic cake

Filling and garnish
1 liter (2 pints) strawberries
sugar
4 dl (2 cups) whipping cream

Save the nicest strawberries for garnish. Mash the rest, about one half, and mix with sugar to taste.

Whip the cream stiff. Mix half of the cream with the mashed berries. Put the cake layers together with the berry cream between.

Cover the entire cake with whipped cream and decorate with strawberries. Chill before serving.

The popular fancy Cream cake may be filled with vanilla custard and covered with lots of whipped cream and fruit. This cake is dusted with grated chocolate.

Punch Cake
Punschtårta

1 quantity basic cake, page 72

Filling and garnish
1 ½ dl (¾ cup) Swedish punch
3 dl (1 ½ cups) whipping cream

Bake the cake in two cake pans. When cool, soak each layer with ½ dl (¼ cup) punch.

Whip the cream stiff and flavor with punch to taste, about ½ dl (¼ cup). Put the layers together with part of the cream between. Cover the entire cake with the remaining cream. Chill well before serving.

Lemon Cake
Citrontårta

1 quantity basic cake, page 72

Lemon cream filling
2 egg whites
2 egg yolks
1 dl (½ cup) sugar
grated rind of ½ lemon
juice of 1 lemon
1 envelope unflavored gelatin
½ dl (¼ cup) water
2 dl (1 cup) whipping cream

Garnish
2 dl (1 cup) whipping cream
candied lemon peel

To make the filling, beat the egg yolks and sugar until light. Add the grated lemon rind and juice. Soften the gelatin in the water and heat, stirring, until liquid. Stir the gelatin into the egg batter and set aside for a couple of minutes, stirring occasionally.

Beat the egg whites stiff. Whip the cream thick. When the egg batter is slightly thickened, fold in the egg whites and cream. Blend well but do not overfold.

Assemble the cake with lemon cream filling between the layers. Cover the top and sides with whipped cream. Garnish with slivers of candied lemon peel. Chill 1 hour or longer before serving.

Fruit Cake
Frukttårta

1 quantity basic cake, page 72
1 quantity vanilla custard filling, page 82

Garnish
7 dl (3 cups) fresh or canned fruit,
  e.g. 1 cup grapes, 1 cup sliced peaches
  and 3 slices pineapple
2 dl (1 cup) prepared lemon-flavored
  gelatin dessert
1 dl (½ cup) whipping cream

Assemble the cake with vanilla custard filling between the layers. Wrap the cake with a 7 cm (3-inch) high collar of aluminum foil. Arrange the fruit on top of the cake. Prepare the gelatin dessert; when almost set, spoon the jelly over the fruit. Let set in refrigerator. Remove the foil. Whip the cream stiff and spread on the side of the cake. Or use a pastry bag and decorate the sides with "ribs" of whipped cream.

Cloudberry Cake
Hjortrontårta

An exquisite fruit from the marshes of northern Sweden the cloudberry looks somewhat like an orange raspberry but has a distinctive, delightful flavor of its own. Look for cloudberry preserve in good Scandinavian food markets.

Layers
1 teaspoon active dry yeast
1 dl (½ cup) sour cream

100 g (4 oz.) butter
3 dl (1 ½ cups) sifted all-purpose flour
  (150 g)
2 tablespoons sugar

Filling
3 dl (1 ½ cups) whipping cream
1 dl (½ cup) cloudberry preserve

In a small bowl, stir together the yeast and sour cream, set aside for 5 minutes. In a large mixing bowl, rub the butter into the flour. When crumbly, add the sour cream mixture. Knead quickly into a rough ball. Cover the bowl and chill for 2 hours.

Preheat oven to 175°C (375°F). Cut the dough in half and roll out each part into a 25 cm (10-inch) circle directly on a large, lightly floured nonstick cookie sheet. Prick with a fork at 1 cm (½-inch) intervals and sprinkle each circle with 1 tablespoon sugar. Set aside for 15 minutes, then bake the layers for 8 to 10 minutes, or till crisp and golden.

Loosen the cakes carefully but leave to cool on the cookie sheet for 5 minutes, then transfer to wire rack to finish cooling.

Whip the cream thick and blend in the cloudberry preserve. This may be done an hour ahead of time; store in refrigerator.

Just before serving, put the layers together with the cloudberry cream between. Use a sharp knife and cut in wedges. Makes 8 servings.

Flarn Cake
Flarntårta

Layers:
100 g (4 oz.) butter
2 dl (1 cup) finely chopped hazelnuts
**   or blanched almonds**
1 dl (½ cup) sugar
2 tablespoons milk
2 tablespoons flour

Filling
1 liter (2 pints) vanilla ice cream or
3 dl (1 ½ cups) whipping cream

Preheat oven to 200°C (400 °F). Butter a
25 cm (10-inch) cast-iron skillet.

In small saucepan, melt the butter. Add
the nuts, sugar, milk and flour. Bring to a
simmer, stirring constantly. Do not let the
mixture boil. Remove from heat.

Spread ⅓ of the batter in the skillet.
Bake for about 10 minutes or until golden
brown. Place the skillet on wire rack and
let cool for a few minutes. Use a long
slender spatula and remove the layer when
somewhat hardened, but before it is too
crisp. Bake two more layers the same way.

Just before serving, assemble the pastry
with ice cream or whipped cream between
the layers. Flavor the cream with rum or
cognac if you like.

The layers may be baked ahead of time.
To retain their crispness, store in container with tight-fitting lid. If desired,
serve the pastry with hot chocolate sauce.
Or spread each layer with melted chocolate before assembling.

Thousand Leaves Cake
Tusenbladstårta

1 quantity basic puff pastry, page 51
2 tablespoons sugar

Filling
4 dl (2 cups) apple sauce
3 tablespoons frozen orange juice,
**   thawed and undiluted**

Garnish
powdered sugar

Prepare the pastry; roll, fold and refrigerate. Divide the pastry in 4 portions. Roll
each part into a 23 cm (9-inch) circle
directly on baking sheet. Prick with a fork
at ½ cm (¼-inch) intervals. Sprinkle with
sugar. Cover and set aside for 30 minutes.

Preheat oven to 225°C (450°F). Bake for
5 to 6 minutes, or until barely golden. Let
cool on baking sheet.

Dust the nicest looking layer with powdered sugar; garnish with fruit or jelly if
you like. Immediately before serving,
assemble the tårta with apple sauce mixed
with orange juice between the layers.

Or use 2 dl apple sauce and 2 dl vanilla
custard.

The pictured Thousand
Leaves Cake is assembled
from square flaky layers with
vanilla custard and apple
sauce between.

Caramel Cake
Kolatårta

3 eggs
2 dl (1 cup) sugar
2 dl (1 cup) sifted all-purpose flour (100 g)
225 g (8 oz.) butter, melted

Filling
1 quantity vanilla custard filling, page 82

Caramel frosting
2 dl (1 cup) whipping cream
1 ¾ dl (⅔ cup) sugar
2 tablespoons dark corn syrup
1 tablespoon cocoa
1 tablespoon butter
1 teaspoon vanilla sugar

Garnish
15 chopped pistachio nuts or hazelnuts

Preheat oven to 175°C (350°F). Butter and flour a 25 cm (10-inch) skillet.

Beat the eggs and sugar until pale and thick. Stir in the flour, then the melted butter. Blend well. Pour the batter into the skillet. Bake for 25 to 30 minutes. Invert the cake and let cool.

To make the frosting, combine the cream, sugar, syrup and cocoa in a saucepan. Let cook, stirring occasionally, on low heat until thick. Put a drop into a glass of cold water; it should solidify. Or test the frosting with a candy thermometer; it should read 125°C (230°F). Stir in the butter and vanilla, let cool.

Split the cake in two layers; use a long thin knife with serrate edge and cut the cake with sawing motions.

Put the layers together with vanilla custard between. Spread the top and the sides with frosting. Sprinkle with nuts on top. Serve at room temperature.

Mocha Cake
Mockatårta

1 quantity basic cake, page 72

Filling and garnish
4 dl (2 cups) whipping cream
2 tablespoons sugar
1 teaspoon instant coffee powder
½ dl (¼ cup) chopped blanched almonds, toasted
½ dl (¼ cup) flaked almonds, toasted

Combine the cream, sugar and coffee powder; beat until stiff. Spread two cake layers with part of the cream and sprinkle with the chopped almonds. Put them together and cover with the third cake layer. Spread the entire cake with the remaining cream. Garnish the top with sliced almonds.

To toast the almonds, spread them on baking sheet and put in a 175°C (350°F) oven for a few minutes.

Arrack Ring
Arrakskrans

This is an old Swedish *"tårta"*.

3 eggs
1 dl (½ cup) sugar
1 ½ dl (⅔ cup) sifted cake or all-purpose
    flour (50 g)
1 teaspoon baking powder

For moistening the cake
2 tablespoons Swedish punch
2 tablespoons water

Butter cream
½ dl (¼ cup) water
1 dl (½ cup) sugar
3 egg yolks
175 g (6 oz.) butter
3 tablespoons Swedish punch

Praline
1 dl (½ cup) sugar
½ dl (¼ cup) coarsely chopped blanched
    almonds

Preheat oven to 175°C (350°F). Butter and
flour a 1 ½ liter (6-cup) ring mold.

Beat the eggs and sugar till thick and
pale. Stir in the flour mixed with baking
powder, blend well. Pour the batter into
the pan. Bake for 15 to 20 minutes.
Unmold and let cool.

To make the butter cream, combine the
water and sugar in small saucepan. Bring
to a boil and cook uncovered until thick
and the syrup spins a thread. To test this,
dip a spoon into the syrup, then into cold
water. Take a drop between your fingers,
part them–the syrup should form a fine
thread. Or test the syrup with a candy
thermometer, it should read 125°C
(230°F).

Beat the egg yolks together, then slowly
add the hot syrup vigorously beating. Let
cool. Stir the butter till creamy and add to
the egg batter a tablespoon at a time, beating well between each addition. Stir in the
punch.

To make the praline, melt the sugar in a
skillet over low heat, stirring constantly.
When light brown and syrupy, add the
chopped almonds. Pour the mixture onto
buttered baking sheet; leave to cool and
harden. Break the praline into pieces and
crush them coarsely with mortar and pestle. Or put them in a plastic bag and roll
with a rolling pin.

Split the cake in two layers. Sprinkle
both halves with punch mixed with water.
Put the layers together with part of the
butter cream between, about ⅓. Spread
the remaining cream over the cake. Coat
the cake with the praline: sprinkle it on
from all sides and gently press it into the
butter cream. Chill the cake before
serving.

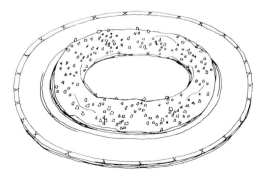

Black Forest Cake
Schwarzwaldtårta

Layers
2 dl (1 cup) hazelnuts
2 dl (1 cup) powdered sugar
4 egg whites

Filling
4 dl (2 cups) whipping cream
¾ dl (⅓ cup) chopped hazelnuts, roasted

Garnish
1 ½ dl (⅔ cup) semi-sweet chocolate morsels, melted
cocoa

Preheat oven to 150°C (325°F). Line three baking sheets with buttered aluminum foil and draw a 23 cm (9-inch) circle on each.

Spread the nuts in a jelly roll pan and roast for a few minutes in oven. Rub the nuts with a cloth to remove the skin. Grind them and mix with the sugar.

Beat the egg whites into stiff peaks. Fold in the nuts and sugar. Spread the circles with the batter. Bake each layer for about 15 minutes, or until light brown. Let cool, then loosen from the foil.

Pour the melted chocolate in a thin layer onto a cookie sheet lined with waxed paper. Cut in 4 cm (1 ½-inch) squares when hardened.

Whip the cream thick and mix with the nuts. Put the layers together with cream between and on top. Spread the sides of the cake with the remaining cream. Stand the chocolate squares around the cake and place a few on top. Sift the top with cocoa. Chill 1 hour before serving.

Raspberry Roll
Hallonrulltårta

3 eggs
1 dl (½ cup) sugar
1 ½ dl (⅔ cup) sifted cake or all-purpose flour (75 g)
1 teaspoon baking powder

Filling and garnish
3 dl (1 ½ cups) whipping cream
1 liter (2 pints) raspberries
sugar

Preheat oven to 225°C (425°F). Line a sheet cake pan, 27 by 40 cm (11 by 16 inches), with buttered aluminum foil.

Beat the eggs and sugar till thick and pale. Mix the flour and baking powder, stir into the egg batter. Blend well. Spread the batter in the pan. Bake for 5 to 6 minutes, or until golden.

Sprinkle the cake with sugar and invert onto wire rack lined with waxed paper. Let the cake cool covered with the pan.

Whip the cream stiff. Mix half of the cream with the berries, saving a handful for garnish. Add sugar to taste and spread over the cold cake. Roll it up, starting from the short side. Cover the roll with remaining cream and garnish with berries.

A homebaked party cake, like this Black Forest Cake, will make any coffee party a success.

Fruit Flan
Mördegstårta

Shell
5 tablespoons butter
½ dl (¼ cup) sugar
1 egg yolk
2 dl (1 cup) sifted all-purpose flour

Vanilla custard filling
2 dl (1 cup) light cream
2 egg yolks
1 tablespoon sugar
2 teaspoons corn starch
1 tablespoon vanilla sugar

Garnish
7 dl (3 cups) fresh or canned fruit,
** e.g. strawberries**
2 dl (1 cup) prepared lemon-flavored
** gelatin dessert**

Preheat oven to 175°C (350°F). Butter a
fluted, false-bottomed 23 cm (9-inch) pan.

Cream the butter, sugar and egg yolk.
Add the flour and work the dough with
your hands until smooth. Press it into the
pan to coat the bottom and the sides in an
even layer. Press a 3 cm (1-inch) wide
strip of aluminum foil along the side to
support it during baking.

Bake for 10 to 15 minutes or until light
golden. Let cool in the pan. Place it on top
of a jar and remove the ring. Place the
shell on serving platter.

To make the filling, combine the
cream, egg yolks, sugar and corn starch in
a saucepan. (Do not use an aluminum pan
unless it has the nonstick finish or your
custard will turn a light greeen.) Bring to a

simmer continuously stirring; cook until
thickened. Let cool, covered, and stir in
the vanilla. (Swedish vanilla sugar can be
obtanined at Scandinavian delicatessen.
Vanilla extract may be used as a substitute.)

Fill the shell with the cold vanilla custard. Arrange the fruit on top. Prepare the
gelatin dessert; when almost set, spoon
the jelly over the fruit. Let set ½ hour in
refrigerator before serving. Makes 8 servings.

Almond Cake
with Punch Sauce
Mandeltårta
med punschsås

The bottom layer for this cake may be
baked a day or two ahead of time; make
the sauce about 1 hour before serving and
store in refrigerator.

225 g (½ lb.) blanched almonds
2 dl (1 cup) sugar
4 egg whites

Garnish
8 canned pear halves, drained
** (or peaches)**
2 tablespoons coarsely grated semi-
** sweet chocolate**

Sauce
4 egg yolks
½ dl (¼ cup) sugar

3 to 4 tablespoons Swedish punch
 (or cognac or rum)
2 dl (1 cup) whipping cream

Preheat oven to 175°C (350°F). Butter a
25 cm (10-inch) skillet or cake pan,
sprinkle with fine dry bread crumbs.

Grind the almonds–use an almond grin-
der or whirl the almonds in electric blender till pulverized. Mix with the sugar.
Beat the egg whites till stiff and fold in the
almond mixture. Spread the batter in skillet. Bake for about 25 minutes or till light
golden. Unmold onto wire rack lined with
wax paper, and let cool covered with the
skillet. Transfer to serving platter and put
the pears on top of the cake. Sprinkle with
the chocolate.

To make the sauce, beat the egg yolks
and sugar till fluffy. Stir in the punch.
Whip the cream thick and blend with the
punch mixture, pour into glass bowl.
Serve the sauce with the cake.
Makes 8 servings.

Chocolate Cake
Chokladtårta

Cake
3 egg whites
3 egg yolks
½ dl (¼ cup) sugar
100 g butter
225 g (8 oz.) almond paste
**150 g (1 cup) semi-sweet chocolate
 morsels, melted**
¾ dl (⅓ cup) sifted all-purpose flour
1 teaspoon baking powder

Filling and garnish
3 dl (1 ½ cups) whipping cream
**½ dl (¼ cup) frozen orange juice, thawed
 and undiluted**
10 apricot halves, drained
10 chopped pistachio nuts

Preheat oven to 175°C (350°F). Butter and
flour two 23 cm (9-inch) cake pans.

Beat the egg whites to a stiff foam.
Work the egg yolks, sugar, butter and
almond paste with your electric beater set
at high speed till creamy and free from
lumps. Stir in the melted chocolate, then
the flour mixed with the baking powder.
Fold in half of the beaten egg whites, then
the other half. Blend until the egg whites
are no longer visible, but do not overfold.

Spread the batter in the cake pans. Bake
for 15 to 18 minutes. Unmold the cakes
and let cool covered with a terry towel.

Whip the cream stiff. Blend with the
orange juice. Assemble the cake with part
of the cream between the layers. Spread
the remaining cream over the top and
sides of the cake. Garnish with apricot
halves curved side up. Sprinkle with
chopped nuts between the apricots.
Chill before serving.

Alexander Cake
Alexandertårta

Shell
175 g (6 oz.) butter
1 dl (½ cup) sugar
1 egg yolk
4 ½ dl (2 cups) sifted all-purpose flour
  (200 g)

Filling I
1 dl (½ cup) apricot or raspberry
  preserve

Filling II
100 g (4 oz.) butter
½ dl (¼ cup) powdered sugar
225 g (8 oz.) almond paste
3 eggs
¾ dl (⅓ cup) sifted all-purpose flour
1 teaspoon baking powder

Glaze
1 tablespoon apricot or raspberry
  preserve

Preheat oven to 175°C (350°F). Butter a 25 cm (10-inch) false-bottomed cake pan.

To make the shell, cream butter and sugar. Stir in the egg yolk. Add the flour and work the dough with your hands until smooth and well blended. Use ⅔ of the dough and press into the cake pan: The dough should cover the bottom and 3 cm (1 ¼-inches) of the side of the pan. Refrigerate the rest of the dough. Spread the bottom with preserve.

Place the butter in mixing bowl and add the sugar and almond paste broken up into pieces. Beat with your electric beater set at high speed till creamy. Add the eggs one at a time beating well after each. Stir in the flour mixed with the baking powder. Spread the filling in the cake pan.

Roll out the refrigerated dough to ¼ cm (⅛-inch) thickness and cut with pastry wheel into 1 cm (½-inch) strips. Place the strips in a lattice pattern on top of the cake. Bake for 35 to 40 minutes, or till a toothpick inserted in center comes out clean. Let cool for 10 minutes. Set on top of a jar and gently push the side of the pan down. Transfer the cake to serving platter. Brush each square with preserve.

This cake is best when newly baked and still a little warm, but it is also very good the second and third days.

Because it is mainly used for this cake, a false-bottomed cake pan is known in Sweden as *Alexanderform* or Alexander pan. Of course, you can use an ordinary cake pan or skillet but the cake must then be left in the pan as it is difficult to unmold without damaging it.

Nut Cake
Nöttårta

Layers
225 g (8 oz.) butter
1 ½ dl (⅔ cup) sugar
1 egg yolk
2 dl (1 cup) hazelnuts
4 dl (2 cups) sifted all-purpose flour
  (200 g)

Frosting
**200 g (1 heaped cup) semi-sweet
  chocolate morsels**

Filling
4 dl (2 cups) whipping cream

Garnish
1 can mandarin oranges, drained

Cream the butter and sugar, stir in the egg
yolk. Grind the nuts and mix with the
flour, add to the dough. Blend until
smooth. Chill the dough 30 minutes. Preheat oven to 175°C (350°F).

Divide the dough in 5 and roll out each
part into a 25 cm (10-inch) circle directly
onto a large baking sheet with nonstick
finish. Bake for 8 to 10 minutes, or until
the edges turn light golden. Leave to cool
on the baking sheet. Sprinkle the hot layers with the chocolate; spread when warm
and melted.

Whip the cream stiff, add sugar if
desired. Assemble the cake with whipped
cream between the layers. Put a ring of
whipped cream on top and decorate with
the fruit. Chill 1 hour before serving.

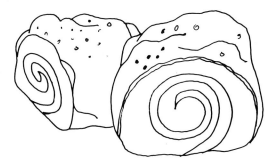

Nut Log
Nötstubbe

Cake
2 dl (1 cup) hazelnuts
**1 dl (½ cup) cake or all-purpose flour
  (50 g)**
1 teaspoon baking powder
3 eggs
1 dl (½ cup) sugar

Filling and garnish
3 dl (1 ½ cups) whipping cream
2 bananas, sliced
**½ dl (¼ cup) coarsely chopped
  roasted hazelnuts**

Preheat oven to 225°C (425°F). Butter a
sheet cake pan 27 by 40 cm (11 by 16
inches) and sprinkle with bread crumbs.

Grind the hazelnuts and mix with the
flour and baking powder. Beat the eggs
and sugar until pale and thick, stir in the
dry ingredients. Blend well. Spread the
batter in the pan. Bake for 5 to 6 minutes,
or until golden.

Sprinkle the cake with sugar and invert
onto a wire rack lined with waxed paper.
Let the cake cool covered with the pan.

Whip the cream stiff. Mix half of the
cream with the sliced bananas and spread
on top of the cold cake. Roll it up from the
long side. Garnish the roll with the
remaining cream and roasted nuts.

To roast the nuts, spread the chopped
nuts on cookie sheet. Roast in a 175°C
(350°F) oven for 4 to 5 minutes or until
light brown, stirring the nuts now and
then.

Bread

Bread is an important part of a Swedish meal. The average Swede eats bread both at breakfast, lunch and dinner.

The last 10 years the interest in bread-baking has risen immensely in Sweden. Today very many, both men and women, are themselves making the bread needed by the household. It gives the family wonderful, fresh, good-tasting bread; you know just what ingredients – no added chemicals, preservatives, colorings or anything else – that have gone into your bread; and it saves money.

The bread used in Sweden is of many different kinds. There is white, so called "French bread", graham bread and rye bread. Bread baked from rye flour has always been very popular with the Swedes. The dry, crispy *knäckebröd* or crispbread, typical of Sweden, is usually made of rye flour. Crispbread is mostly store-bought but some even make this bread themselves.

Many Swedes are health-conscious today and make their bread with part wholemeal flour and without adding sugar or syrup. The sweetened *limpa* or light rye loaf may still be the bread favored by most though.

The growing interest in bread baking has led to the development of a whole new line of different flours and flour mixes. As these cannot be obtained outside Sweden, they are not used in this book. To make the kinds of bread presented here, you will use standard all-purpose flour, rye flour and graham flour. Measure the rye flour and all-purpose flour by sifting into the cup, then leveling off. Do not sift graham flour – spoon it into the measuring cup. If the dough is sticky after you have added all the flour, gradually add some more.

To dissolve dry yeast in water of the right temperature, follow the instructions on the package. Fresh yeast should always be dissolved in *lukewarm* water (body temperature, 37°C (or 98°F).

Kneading is necessary if you want a nice tasting, high loaf with a smooth crust. If you don't knead the dough properly, the bread will be flatter, the crumb will have a rough structure and the crust will not be as attractive.

Always bake your bread in the lower third of the oven, if not otherwise stated.

Limpa

1 envelope active dry yeast
    or 50 g (2 oz.) fresh yeast
2 dl (1 cup) warm water
50 g (2 oz.) butter
2 dl (1 cup) milk
½ tablespoon anise or fennel seed,
    crushed
1 teaspoon salt
2 tablespoons dark corn syrup
4 dl (2 cups) sifted rye flour (200 g)
about 1 liter (5 cups) sifted all-purpose
    flour (500 g)

In large mixing bowl, dissolve the yeast in the warm water. In small saucepan, melt the butter. Add the milk to the saucepan and heat until lukewarm, then add the mixture to the yeast. Stir in the anise or fennel, salt and syrup. Gradually work in the rye flour and all-purpose flour. Blend well, then cover and leave to rise for 1 hour.

Turn dough onto lightly floured surface. Knead well until smooth. Shape the dough into two 23 cm (9-inch) loaves and place on baking sheet. Cover and let rise till double, about 1 hour.

Prick the loaves with a fork. Bake in a preheated 175°C (350°F) oven for 35 to 40 minutes. Knock the bread on the bottom and you should hear a hollow sound. If not, return bread to oven. Brush the top of the loaves with warm water. Wrap them in terry towels and let cool on rack. Makes 2 loaves.

Flat Rye Bread
Hålkakor

Prepare the dough as for Limpa and let rise. Knead well and divide into 4 portions. Shape each portion into a round ball and roll into a flat 20 cm (8-inch) circle. Use the cap from a bottle and cut a hole in center. Place the bread on baking sheet and prick with a fork at 2 cm (1-inch) intervals. Cover and let rise till double.

Bake in preheated 175°C (375°F) oven for 15 to 18 minutes. Brush with warm water and let the bread cool covered with cloths. To serve, cut in wedges and split the wedges in half. Makes 4 rounds.

Flat, round bread, "hålkakor", is served cut in wedges which are split in half horizontally.

Wort Limpa
Vörtlimpa

This is the classic Swedish Christmas bread used for the traditional Dip or *dopp i grytan:* slices of wort limpa are immersed in hot bouillon, then enjoyed steaming hot with ham or sausage.

Wort can sometimes be obtained from large breweries, otherwise stout or porter is a good substitute.

If you can't find pomeransskal (see page 11), leave it out.

1 envelope active dry yeast
   or 50 g (2 oz.) fresh yeast
1 dl (½ cup) warm water
2 dl (1 cup) wort or stout
1 teaspoon salt
4 dl (2 cups) sifted rye flour (200 g)
2 dl (1 cup) sifted all-purpose flour (100 g)
1 pomeransskal
50 g (2 oz.) butter
½ dl (¼ cup) dark corn syrup
½ tablespoon ginger
½ tablespoon cloves
about 4 dl (2 cups) sifted all-purpose flour (200 g)

In large mixing bowl, dissolve the yeast in the warm water. Heat the wort till tepid and add to the yeast together with the salt, rye flour and 1 cup all-purpose flour. Mix well. Cover and leave to rise for 1 hour.

Cook the pomeransskal in water until soft. Remove and discard the white part, chop the yellow peel finely. In small saucepan, melt the butter. Stir in the syrup and spices, cool until lukewarm and add to the dough together with the chopped peel. Gradually stir in the all-purpose flour. Cover and let rise for ½ hour.

Turn the dough onto ligthly floured surface and knead well until smooth. Shape the dough into a 30 cm (12-inch) loaf and place on baking sheet. Cover and leave to rise till double. Prick the top of the bread with a fork and bake in preheated 175°C (350°F) oven for 35 to 40 minutes. A knock on the bottom of the bread should produce a hollow sound. Brush the top of the limpa with wort mixed with liquid from cooking the pomeransskal. Wrap the bread in terry towels and let cool on rack. Makes 1 loaf.

Kubb

Here is a traditional, very special Swedish bread. Dark and dense, the kubb has a good rye flavor; it is best served in thin slices with butter.

1 envelope active dry yeast
   or 50 g (2 oz.) fresh yeast
3 dl (1 ½ cups) warm water
1 teaspoon salt
2 dl (1 cup) dark corn syrup
8 dl (4 cups) sifted rye flour (400 g)
about 8 dl (4 cups) sifted all-purpose flour (400 g)

In large mixing bowl, dissolve the yeast in the warm water. Add the salt, syrup and rye flour, mix well. Gradually stir in the all-purpose flour. Turn the dough onto lightly floured surface and knead until smooth and shiny.

Shape the dough into a ball and place in buttered 1 ½ kg (3-lb.) coffee can or other can of similar shape. Cover and leave to rise at room temperature till double, 4 to 5 hours.

Cover the can tightly with aluminum foil. Place it in large, deep kettle and fill with water up to ⅔ the height of the can. Cook for 4 hours in preheated 175°C (350°F) oven. Replace the water as needed.

When baked, turn out the bread and let cool wrapped in terry towels. To serve, cut the bread lengthwise into 4 wedges and slice each wedge across. Makes 1 loaf.

White Bread
Vitt formbröd

25 g (1 oz.) fresh yeast
5 dl (2 ½ cups) warm milk
2 teaspoons salt
2 tablespoons oil
about 1.4 liter (7 cups) all-purpose flour (700 g)

In large mixing bowl, dissolve the yeast in the milk. Add salt and oil. Gradually stir in the flour. Stir till well blended. Cover the bowl and leave to rise for 1 hour.

Turn dough onto lightly floured surface. Add more flour if needed. Knead well until smooth.

Cut off a portion as big as your fist. Shape the rest of the dough into a loaf and put it in greased bread pan (2 liter or 9 cups).

Divide the small piece of dough into 3 portions and roll into strands. Make a thin plait and place it along the top of the loaf.

Cover and leave to rise for about 45 minutes. Bake in a 225°C (425°F) oven for about 30 minutes. Turn out the bread and let it cool on a rack uncovered. Makes 1 loaf.

White Poppy Bread
Bergis

Note that white bread can also be baked directly on a greased baking sheet. Brush with beaten egg and sprinkle with poppy seeds. (See photo on page 92–93).

This white bread strewn
with poppy seeds is as tasty
as it is beautiful to look at.
The Swedish name for it is
"Bergis" (page 91).

Tea Rolls
Tekakor

The name does not mean a thing – these rolls are good any time. Split in half horizontally they are often used for open-face sandwiches.

**1 envelope active dry yeast
   or 50 g (2 oz.) fresh yeast
½ dl (¼ cup) warm water
2 tablespoons butter
2 dl (1 cup) milk
1 teaspoon salt
1 tablespoon sugar
about 8 dl (4 cups) sifted all-purpose
   flour (400 g)**

In large mixing bowl, dissolve the yeast in the warm water. In small saucepan, melt the butter. Add the milk to the saucepan and heat until lukewarm, then add this mixture to the yeast. Stir in the salt, sugar and half of the flour. Gradually add the remaining flour. Work the dough until well blended. Cover the bowl and leave to rise for 1 hour.

Turn the dough onto lightly floured surface and knead well until smooth and shiny. Divide the dough into 12 parts and shape into round balls. Roll each ball with rolling pin into a 10 cm (4-inch) circle. Place the rolls on baking sheet and prick with a fork. Cover and leave to rise till double. Bake in preheated 225°C (425°F) oven for about 10 minutes. Brush with warm water and let the rolls cool covered with a cloth. Makes 12.

The same dough may be used for Hot Dog Rolls. Follow the recipe but shape into 15 cm (6-inch) sticks.

Rye Sticks
Rågpainriche

**25 g (1 oz.) fresh yeast
2 teaspoons salt
5 dl (2 ½ cups) warm water
5 dl (2 ½ cups) rye flour (250 g)
about 9 dl (4 ½ cups) all-purpose flour
   (450 g)**

In large mixing bowl, dissolve the yeast in the warm water. Add the salt and the rye flour. Gradually add the all-purpose flour. Blend well, then cover and leave to rise for 1 hour.

Turn dough onto lightly floured surface. Add more flour if needed. Knead well until smooth.

Divide dough into 6 portions. Shape each portion into a stick as long as the long side of the baking sheet. Put the sticks, three and three, on greased baking sheets.

If you like, cut the dough with scissors or make diagonal cuts with a sharp knife.

Cover and leave to rise at room temperature till almost double in size, about 1 hour.

Bake in the middle of a 250°C (475°F) oven about 12 minutes or until nicely colored. Let the bread cool on rack uncovered.

To serve, cut the bread-sticks in 7 cm (3-inch) pieces and divide them horizontally. Makes 6.

Two-Day Bread
Skållat bröd

When wholemeal flour is scalded with boiling water and then left to stand at room temperature for about a day, the resulting bread gets an extra nice taste and consistency. This kind of bread will also keep fresh for a longer time than ordinary bread.

Day 1
7 dl (3 ½ cups) boiled water
2 dl (1 cup) wheat bran
4 dl (2 cups) rye flour (200 g)

Day 2
5 dl (2 ½ cups) warm water
50 g (2 oz.) fresh yeast
½ dl (¼ cup) oil

1 tablespoon salt
1.5 liter (7 cups) graham flour (900 g)
5 dl (2 ½ cups) rye flour (250 g)
about 1 liter (5 cups) all-purpose flour (500 g)

Day 1: Boil the water in a large pan. Take it from the heat and stir in the bran and rye flour. Cover with the lid. Let stand in the kitchen until next day.
Day 2: Add the warm water to the pan. Crumble the yeast into the pan; add oil and salt. Stir until well blended.

Add the graham flour. Gradually stir in the all-purpose flour. Cover and leave dough to rise in the pan 1 hour.

Turn dough onto lightly floured surface. Knead well and divide into 2 parts. Shape them into loaves. Place them both in a greased sheet cake-pan. Brush the sides of the loaves with oil and they can easily be separated after baking.

Cover and leave to rise for 1 hour. Bake at 175°C (350°F) for 1 hour. Turn out the bread, wrap in terry towels and let cool on rack. Do not cut the bread until next day.

Karlsbader Rolls
Karlsbaderbröd

1 envelope active dry yeast
**   or 50 g (2 oz.) fresh yeast**
½ dl (¼ cup) warm water
2 dl (1 cup) light cream
1 teaspoon sugar
1 teaspoon salt
3 egg yolks
about 8 dl (4 cups) sifted all-purpose flour (400 g)
100 g (4 oz.) butter, softened

In large mixing bowl, dissolve the yeast in the warm water. Stir in the cream, sugar, salt and egg yolks. Blend in half of the flour, then add the softened butter and blend well. Stir in the remaining flour. Turn the dough onto lightly floured surface and knead until smooth. The dough will feel quite sticky. Put it in plastic bag and refrigerate for 30 minutes.

Return dough to floured surface and knead briefly. Shape into 18 oblong balls and place on baking sheet. Cover and let rise till double.

Brush the rolls with beaten egg. Bake in preheated 225°C (425°F) oven for about 10 minutes or until golden brown. Makes 18.

Graham Rusks
Grahamsskorpor

Here they are–the world's crispest rusks. Serve them spread with honey or marmalade.

**2 envelopes active dry yeast
  or 100 g (4 oz.) fresh yeast
1 dl (½ cup) warm water
225 g (8 oz.) butter
3 dl (1 ½ cups) milk
1 teaspoon salt
1 tablespoon sugar
6 dl (3 cups) graham flour (400 g)
about 6 dl (3 cups) sifted all-purpose
  flour (300 g)**

In large mixing bowl, dissolve the yeast in the warm water. In small saucepan, melt the butter. Stir in the milk and pour the lukewarm mixture into the yeast. Stir in the salt, sugar and graham flour. Add the all-purpose flour and work the dough until well blended.

Turn the dough onto lightly floured surface and knead well. Divide into 4 portions, then cut each portion into 8 pieces. Roll into smooth oblong balls and place on baking sheet. Cover and let rise till double.

Bake in preheated 250°C (450°F) oven for 10 to 12 minutes. Let cool on rack. Split the rolls with a fork and spread the halves on baking sheet. Toast them in a 200°C (400°F) oven for 12 minutes or till brown. Set the oven door slightly ajar with a wooden spoon and leave the rusks to dry at 75°C (200°F), for about 10 hours or overnight. Makes 64.

Graham Bread
Grahamsbröd

**1 envelope active dry yeast
  or 50 g (2 oz.) fresh yeast
7 dl (3 cups) warm water
½ tablespoon salt
½ dl (¼ cup) dark corn syrup
1 dl (½ cup) raisins (optional)
6 dl (3 cups) graham flour (400 g)
about 9 dl (4 ½ cups) sifted all-purpose
  flour (450 g)**

In large mixing bowl, dissolve the yeast in the warm water. Stir in the salt, syrup, raisins and graham flour. Add the all-purpose flour a cup at a time and work the dough until well blended. Cover and let rise for about 1 hour.

Turn the dough onto lightly floured surface and knead well. Divide the dough in two portions and shape into loaves. Place them in buttered 1 ½ liter (6-cup) bread pans. Cover and let rise for 1 hour or till doubled.

Bake in preheated 175°C (375°F) oven for 50 to 60 minutes. Unmold the loaves and brush the top with warm water. Wrap in terry towels and let cool on rack. Makes 2 loaves.

Rusks made of graham flour are tender and delicious with butter and marmalade.

Coffee Table Suggestions

A Christmas Coffee Table

Christmas and baking are inseparable. Even Swedes who never bake during the rest of the year will bake something at Christmas, such as a few festive holiday cookies or perhaps a special cake, using an old family recipe. Here are two suggestions for a traditional Christmas coffee table:

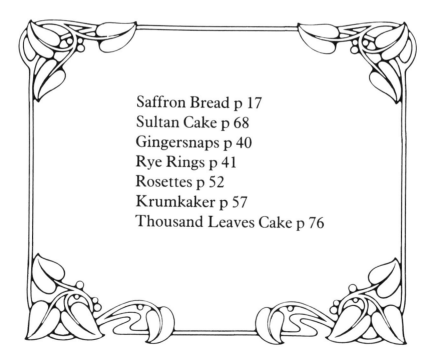

Saffron Bread p 17
Sultan Cake p 68
Gingersnaps p 40
Rye Rings p 41
Rosettes p 52
Krumkaker p 57
Thousand Leaves Cake p 76

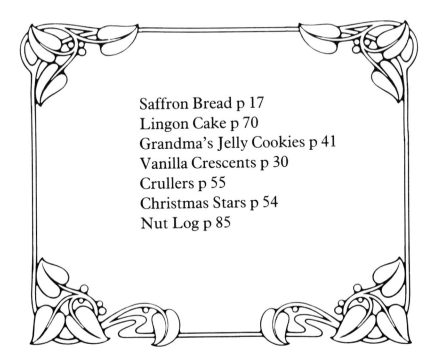

A Swedish Coffee Party

Kafferep, when women get together to drink coffee and to talk, is the Swedish equivalent of the American coffee clutch. In the Swedish countryside, the kafferep is still an honored tradition. If you want to gather your friends to a real, old-fashioned kafferep, here are two suggestions.

Seven is the magic number for the coffee table; if you want to be traditional, there must be seven kinds of goodies served with the coffee.

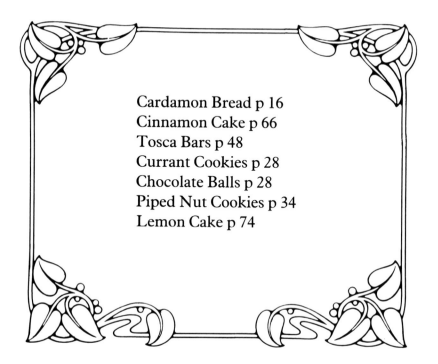

Cardamon Bread p 16
Cinnamon Cake p 66
Tosca Bars p 48
Currant Cookies p 28
Chocolate Balls p 28
Piped Nut Cookies p 34
Lemon Cake p 74

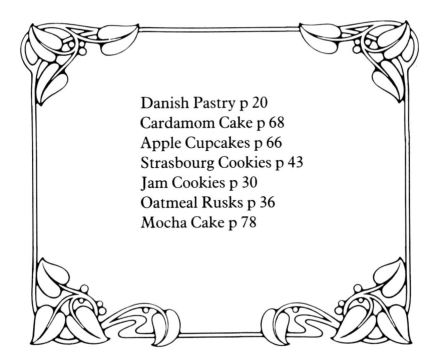

A Children's Party

Orange Cupcakes p 67
Dream Cookies p 36
Caramel Cake p 78
or
Nut Crescents p 22
Coconut Cookies p 44
Filled Pastry Cones p 62

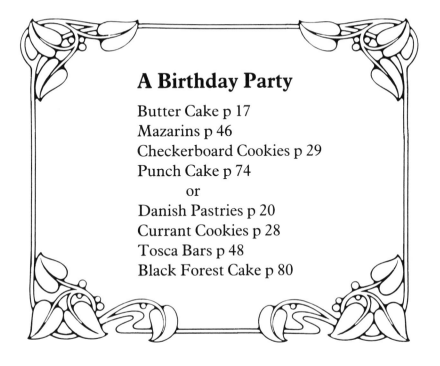

A Birthday Party

Butter Cake p 17
Mazarins p 46
Checkerboard Cookies p 29
Punch Cake p 74
     or
Danish Pastries p 20
Currant Cookies p 28
Tosca Bars p 48
Black Forest Cake p 80

A Midsummer Coffee Table

Almond Rolls p 21
Raisin Cupcakes p 67
Piped Cookies p 33
Strawberry Cake p 72
or
Cardamom Bread p 16
Jam Cookies p 30
Spice Cake p 66
Fruit Flan p 82

A Wedding Reception

Vanilla Hearts p 60
Parisian Cookies p 30
Arrack Ring p 79
           or
Almond Chocolate Pastries p 57
Lemon Rings p 28
Nut Log p 85

Recipe Index, English

Recipe Index, Swedish

General Index